Ash Dîvan

ASH DÎVAN

SELECTED POEMS
of ENIS BATUR

❧

translated by

Clifford Endres   Saliha Paker
Selhan Savcıgil-Endres   Mel Kenne

and a translation of "Digenis"
by Coşkun Yerli and Ronald Tamplin

edited by Saliha Paker

Talisman House, Publishers
Jersey City, New Jersey

Grateful acknowledgment is made for the generous support given to the
publication of this book by the Turkish Ministry of Culture.

ISBN: 1-58498-049-4

First Edition

Published by
Talisman House, Publishers
P.O. Box 3157
Jersey City, New Jersey 07303-3157

Manufactured in the United Sates of America
Printed on acid-free paper

CONTENTS

[v]

III. from *Papirüs, Mürekkep, Tüy* (Papyrus, Ink, Quill) 2002

ACKNOWLEDGEMENTS

Grateful acknowledgment is made to the publishers and editors of the books and journals in which some of these translations first appeared: *An Anthology of Turkish Literature* (ed. Kemal Silay, University of Indiana, 1996), *The Atlanta Review, Agenda, Contemporary Turkish Culture, Eda: An Anthology of Contemporary Turkish Poetry* (ed. Murat Nemet-Nejat, Talisman House, 2004), *Journal of Literature and Aesthetics, The Massachusetts Review, Nar '96, Near East Review, Quarterly West, Seneca Review, Talisman, Translation Review, Turkish Area Studies Review*, and *Cultural Horizons: Festschrift in Honor of Talat Sait Halman* (ed. Jayne L. Warner, Syracuse University Press & YKT, 2001).

PRONUNCIATION GUIDE

â as in *a*lm

c as in *j*ug

ç as in *ch*urch

ğ merely lengthens a vowel that precedes it

î as in *ee*l

ı as in *a*live

ö as in *ea*rly

ş as in *sh*ell

ü as in French *u*ne

Ash Dîvan

A CONCAVE CONVERSATION

By Enis Batur

— The dialogue you've just started brings to mind Montale's "Fictional Interview" of 1946, on which a French poet remarked, "Montale's poetry can best be introduced by Montale himself." Why have you chosen to hand over Ariadne's thread to the reader yourself, while it might have been more appropriate for someone else to preface your *Selected Poems?*

> It was at my publisher's request. Besides, I value Montale very highly as a poet. So I won't pretend I'm unfamiliar with his writing, or, for that matter, with Gide's "Fictional Interviews" that were published in 1943. No doubt you know that I never keep back from recalling my forerunners. With that in mind, we could go as far back as Petrarch, or even farther; the inner dialogue has a long and complicated history. In Montale's interview questions were left blank, but here at least you hold the right to ask what you like, how you like. Certainly, I would've preferred someone else to write a preface or introduction. However, you will remember the prevailing judgment here in Turkey that readers may be separated into those who like Enis Batur and those who don't. I'm not responsible for this view but one has to admit that it is largely true. So I hope you'll agree that I'd be justifiably concerned about a preface tending towards unmeasured praise or disparagement.

Moreover, no poetry is, or can ever be, for everybody. Poets must know and accept that while they fill a gap in the world of some readers,

[3]

they will wound others. This is what experience has taught me since my first book of poetry came out in 1973.

— Perhaps you can also throw some light on another topic: according to some, your work holds a special place in the development of Turkish poetry, particularly of the last quarter of a century. But there are also others who consider you alien and outside the mainstream. Can you tell me where your poetry stands?

> Here, I have to remind my Anglophone reader of where my poetry stands in Turkey's "cultural map." This country of ours has one foot in the Western world, the other in the Eastern. I belong to a society which, in a land marked by ancient Anatolian civilizations, — the Ionian and the Byzantine, the Seljukid and the Ottoman — has been trying, for almost two hundred years, to maintain its aim for Westernization and that of keeping to its traditions. It is true that I've been brought up almost like a European and that I am an agnostic. It is also true that I've been influenced by all religious cultures. At least one fundamental dimension of my poetic sensibility can be connected to the Mediterranean. Despite moving around quite often with a passion for foreign lands and cities, most of all for Paris, I have spent the greater part of my life in Istanbul. As a person, I have no racial or religious feelings of belonging. When asked, I say I live in Istanbul and am passionate about Turkish. This much has sufficed for some to consider me a stranger in my own country. Many others, who appraise poetry in terms of poetry, have given a privileged position to my work in the wake of the "Second New."

Collective enterprises were dominant in Turkish poetry for over half a century. The "Second New," which marked the years 1955-75, was viewed as the most recent one to have created a new, refreshing language. But in its wake, things became difficult for poets. Holding a place within or opposite a movement has a comforting side to it, according to those who are eager to classify; but beginning with my generation, every poet has had to be measured in terms of his or her own career.

— I didn't get a precise answer to my question. You seem to be talking in circles. Where does your work stand in relation to Turkish poetry?

> Bear with me! How can you expect poets to appraise their own poetry or to determine its "place"? You would see that this is not an easy business for others either, if you looked at what has already been written about me. Some critics have claimed that I extended modern Turkish poetry's line of development, others, that I started a breakaway course, still others, that mine was an outsider's trajectory. In a way, I think I've responded to all such views in my "Ars Poetica"; so, again, the answer to your question may be found in my poetry.

— You've just said that you "never kept back from recalling" your "forerunners." Indeed, in the interviews given at different times, you've mentioned some Turkish and foreign sources of influence on your poetry. But it's a bit difficult for me to understand how it has been possible for you to cultivate interest in poets so unlike one another. Pound and Rilke?

Góngora and Mallarmé? Karacaoğlan and Dağlarca? Isn't there some inconsistency in this wide range?

> First of all, my range of poets is actually much wider! I consider myself the natural heir to every good poem written before me. Please don't think of my words as the expression of an infinitely tolerant attitude. I've spent much time studying poets whom I don't feel close to, such as Eliot and Valéry — I still do. Secondly, I must add that philosophy, mysticism, music, the visual arts, and history are serious contributing sources. I seem to have set up my relationship with life and the world in this way; my poetry is abundantly equipped with references, a fact which has been a problem for the reader. Perhaps I should explain my relationship to diverse poets with widely different poetics in this way: my work has moved in three separate directions — lyric, epic, and dramatic; all are governed by the same tone and style, but each genre has followed a different course. For the most part, the lyric is condensed and abstract, while the dramatic is covert and fabulatory. As for the epic, in it an uncurbed stream of prophetic mutterings runs uppermost. I have to say that this three-part division has always been my choice; I never thought harnessing all three inclinations to a single course would work for me. But neither did it cross my mind to give up any one of them. It seems to me that I would never have been able to find correspondences to the flow of the age in which I live in any other way. The lyric branch has called for listening rigorously to Góngora or Karacaoğlan, to Rilke or Char. The whole expressionist tradition serves as a touchstone for my dramatic poems. For the epic, I've had to look at Khlebnikov or Pound with a

[6]

magnifying glass. In short, where you find contradiction, I see a kind of inevitability.

— This selection does not carry any of the poems you wrote before you were thirty. Is this how you wanted it to be? I have another reason for asking this. It seems to me that your earlier poems can be characterized as more savage and reckless, while in your subsequent poetry there is a calming down, even an inclination towards self-domestication. Can we say that you were aspiring to be a "master"?

> First of all I have to tell you that Saliha Paker, the editor, is responsible for the selection of poems. Of course, she always kept in touch with me and asked for my opinion, but it seemed natural to let her have the final say over the choice of the poems. Besides, the selection process was no doubt served by the opinions and preferences of the other translators involved in the project, Clifford Endres, Selhan Endres, and Mel Kenne. I can say that I'm happy with the whole that has emerged from what is, after all, a selection.

To a certain extent, I share your observations on my work. A harsh, if not savage, stance and style may have been dominant in my early poems. When I reached thirty, a part of me felt exhausted with what I had experienced in my twenties. The poems in *Sarnıç* served as a cross-roads. The present selection takes off just there, at that juncture, which, in my view, is the right starting point. Translations of the earlier poems may follow in the future.

[7]

You may remember that several critics, led by the poet Melih Cevdet Anday, had commented on the "prophetic voice," the "messianic tone" that has found a place in my poems. That voice became prominent in the *Sarnıç* (1985) collection. Yes, of course it is possible to go on about calming down and being domesticated, which others have commented on; but coming to rest, gaining clarity, the deeply reaching voice can also be taken as a point of departure. Obviously, you approach the subject of "being a master" with some irony. But perhaps you shouldn't. What we do isn't all that different from making a table or a chair; it is a *métier*. The apprentice's playfulness may be fine, but eventually he too will strive for perfection in making a table. On the other hand, "being a master" has no guarantee, nor a single degree to mark it. From one poem to the next, the poet will climb up his or her own hill.

— Doesn't the fact that you're perceived as a central figure in the "intelligentsia" play a part in the influence of your poetry in Turkey and in the reaction rallied against it? Don't you, as a poet, feel more comfortable when you're translated into other languages?

> That is true. When a book of my poetry is published in Turkey today, the name on the cover has, alas, too many implications. Considering this the outcome not just of what I've written but of what I've done, I can only conclude that my sins must be many! Outside Turkey it's the opposite: the name on the cover appears uncomplicated to the reader. In Italy, Iran or France, as a translated poet I'm not an obstacle between poetry and its reader, but in my own country, I've never enjoyed that freedom.

[8]

— Doesn't your social position, no doubt inflated by the written press and the media, contradict the *abdal* figure that travels through your poetry? Or better still, isn't it at odds with your identity as a poet? Don't you think of it as a huge paradox?

> I happen to be a product of the paradox you've just pronounced. In a youthful poem of mine I had once proposed, "I am two." You may take that as an early confession. Despite my social position you've just referred to, I am known as a person who generally keeps to himself and spends his days mostly in his room. One who webs himself into four walls and spins himself in between them, must be on a long and lonely kind of journey. You can regard this as a split identity, or identify it as a type of personality formed by two contrary "conditions," one the reverse face of the other — that's up to you. Outside, I see myself as a "modern" man, inside, a mystic one. One acts, intervenes, manipulates; the other is introverted, somewhat fugitive, mostly wounded, dependent on writing, on constructing it. Every poet is a flâneur, a wanderer, an *abdal*.

-- How do you build a poem?

> Generally, I don't go to a poem, but wait and ready myself for it to come to me. The rest is a matter of work which requires labor at the desk. Following Octavio Paz, I fill up the interval between two poems with prose. Poetry springs from a certain mood of the spirit but takes its momentum from preparing a voice. I flow in some seasons, but freeze in others. Sometimes I fear it may not come, but it does.

[9]

-- You have some poems on the theme of "translation" and you have translated poetry yourself. What do you think of the translations in this selection?

> Even having my poetry read, let alone translated, alerts me to danger, leaves me in shivers. I get locked up inside, feeling anxious that the music, if not the meaning, might be misunderstood. If one dimension of the translated poem belongs to me, the other belongs to the translator. Translating poetry has mostly to do with a feeling of devotion; you can't do it without love, which is the shortest-cut to reading "right." When I read through the present book, I saw "my" world and heard "my" voice flowing into a foreign tongue, reflecting there. I think this is a rare achievement. My poems have their own secrets, of course. And Turkish, like all languages, displays certain features that allow possibilities for the poet but impose impossibilities on the translator: in what other language *güller güler*?

Everything considered, this book goes with my blessing.

SP

MODERN TIMES

Papyrus, ink, quill.
Toward the core of a somber era
a humming wells up within me from root to summit,
I unroll a map, its infinite scale
covering the earth with its skies and the firmament,
a map for mountains, valleys and seas
inland, dead or open; a chart for my dervish face
that roams through hills and glades,
for my *abdal* voice and hermit gaze.
I am flâneur, wanderer, vagabond saint,
my wonder unsurpassable: where's my home,
where's the mute desert memorial I raised
for my lord whom I've slain, where are the children of night
that I've borne ceaselessly: I descend on myself,
suddenly, like a nightmare or a downpour
of rain, uncalled-for: overflowing all,
making all overflow.

My twin, my double, my mirror:
in the wind that flips calendar pages into a void
the era crumbles, days and nights get confused.
Clocks stop and can't be reset
to that precise balance between the conflicting faces
of the scorpio hour-hand and the minute-chaser.

The screw no longer fits into the groove,
a verb lingers on the tip of my tongue, inside me
a great bird, swift, sharp, quiet, readies its wings,
on the brink of a flight of no return,
in pain, with some pride, it gazes
at the infinite arithmetic of horizons unfolding before it,
it shoots forth like an arrow from the skyline behind,
without spreading its wings
speeding away from gravity
with the invisible strength of its unseen source.

A bird
over babbling human islands
watches the unrelieved aching
of the wounded, crippled, helpless crowd:
the city: is it Paradise or a stream of frozen sewage,
the bird can't tell. Festering pustules
burst open, millions of tiny mercury beads scatter:
as they pull, brush against, push one another
in each the shroud shreds from end to end.

Above workshops like tombs,
djinned stationery in innumerable stacks,
giant cooking pots, spoons in the thousands,
forks, all left sticky in pools, above the sterile
smell of mosquito nets hanging heavily in bedrooms,

above hospital garbage dumps
filled with the unbelievable clatter of syringes,
above gothic skeletons clamped in seagulls' beaks,
above flies, locusts, keenings, laughter and screams
the bird soars, as do I.

There's a tempting outlook that I can't share:
perhaps I landed smack in the middle of life
and the spirit I've strained through my eyes for years,
alloyed with matter, bled away my ordeal
even in the hollow grotto of my retreat.
I've known men who, like flaccid dreams,
turned into bags of flesh and bone,
only tattoo and seal, passing the years.
I've known women, both new and ancient:
each one a full moon, that bright,
each one so much a temporary tale of oblivion.
Children: like a bursting boil,
the nation of hopelessness swelled with them.
I thought it had all changed, but nothing had really
in this room where I stand riveted.

Does the kite I set flying years ago
on the stubborn morning, broken free,
before concrete mulberry trees
had yet been planted in the compassionate earth,

still pursue for eternity its sworn love?
Has my brother who set out on a journey
with a bit of haste, a bit of food and countless
dream-seeds stuffed in his saddle-bag,
arrived at the oasis we all know can never be reached?
I'm here, still waiting for the call
that a weary messenger
will deliver.

Tell me, oh unmoving face,
empty cage that sits waiting,
no longer sure of what to expect:
what we're living through here, now,
is it marching back to yesterday or onward to tomorrow?
Out there, in the directions we haven't tried before,
on an island not infected by disease,
in a lair or on a misty summit,
can we meet one day?
How long, brothers and sisters, and where
have you been keeping that sheer, unaltered light?
Are you still in the cave, blind body, blind shadow,
have you buried the immutable gold
behind those high walls constructed in dreams by sleep?
Here I am asking questions,
emptying and filling a bundle, day and night:

the way is long and the leader once torn away from me
will not return, this much I know.

Is there no echo for the unspoiled stranger?
With a knot in my hand I can't untie,
I can't light a fire to turn my face toward
with what's here on my saddle:
papyrus, quill, ink.
Something's still missing, a suffix,
on the tip of my severed tongue
perhaps a complex noun phrase:
I haven't slept for years, I've tested my senses
in endless work, given up on my organs, let them run dry:
among you alone I flew and cleansed my blood:
I am a deserted boat that calls
on quaysides overflowing with huge crowds.

SP-MK

A TALISMAN AND TRAGEDY

At one end of this pencil lies Tragedy,
at the other a Talisman. As I slept,
who awoke inside me, who went on daydreaming,
which of my faces was bleeding, why did
I just then choose to sharpen one end
while my instincts grew blunt at the other,
at one end of the pencil, Tragedy, on the one
nearest me, a Talisman: turned either way
lay anger born of sadness born of anger:
and at each end of the pencil my flock
of mountain swifts was gathering stones.

With the future's angel left behind me
and my notebook full, I only keep busy now
polishing a hesitant couplet for my headstone.
I crossed bridges, strode through dungeons and tunnels,
my sons are a nation of rebels and each daughter
has become a seed attuned to eternal searching.
This woman I'd loved: she broke out of my world,
a light blown out. I'd loved that one too:
just couldn't get my fill of her.
And, oh yes, she: the one who lived at my side,
like a storm, and who died, sheer muslin.

Now I'm alone, living the way I used to,
a brooding falcon.

My notebook's full: I verged on but didn't attain.
Perhaps I walked through the midpoint of pain,
tangent to serenity's pole, away from my destination.
Saving the unique for myself, I hurt.
Then came the day when outer harmony
was withheld from me by ingrown venom:
in a dark, sly time of stabbing, I took the words
and, one by one, broke them up in my hands.

Then it was all gone, only I was left
with errors and truths in open rebellion against me:
a fragile balance, a steep flight of stairs,
some broken-down hour-glasses,
a compass whose language I'd forgotten,
and those strange animals that shared my nights:
scorpion and spider, salamander and falcon,
and the flock of mountain swifts gathering stones.
The great flood inside me lay at rest
while I gazed upon nature but swelled up
when I turned toward woman or man;
my flights were infrequent and untutored,
I shied away from the stinging burn,
could even hear the slip of a single syllable

on the tongue, I dug a pit and lay in wait
for the absolute prey to be released in it.

Thus began an inexorable ascent
that loomed always before me: I was deluded
maybe, perhaps convinced, yet I never believed
in any sign that left heart and mind unseared.
I remained here, at all times ready to strike
the tent I'd just pitched, to start out on a journey:
in between needle and net, silk and story, fog and foam,
in one notebook after another I wrote my account:
I sought for but couldn't find the golden meaning,
yet I guessed the underlying sense of gold
one night when, awaking in blood,
I sharpened the other end to a fine point:

around me lie dead objects that still stir:
if I touch them, they'll translate all
that they know of me into their own language:
it was *I* who had this clock stopped,
it was *I* who slipped off this ring,
why did I pack in the glass lampshade
I'd shattered on purpose with the one
that had cracked in another's hands?
Here's my desk, my blotting paper, a pair
of bone dice that have kept me company

since I was a child. Here on the wall

the lifeless pictures, on the floor the brownish-gray rug,

beside my bed an opaline lamp,

fathomless notebooks in black leather:

at my touch, the sheer panic sunk into this room over the years

breaks into speech:

I need a purer, more refined light,

a slightly darker ink, a more gripping paralysis

in my right hand and fingers,

I need a bit more time to travel through that time:

a shade more presumption, and fear, maybe,

to last for a few more breaths or longer than a century,

I need a Talisman and Tragedy.

SP-MK

THE CHEST

A box of keys. Régie des Tabacs
de l'Empire Ottomane, flecks of rust,
holes in the sides, it's hard to gauge
this box's weight. Chests of drawers,
file cabinets, houses — their owners
just ghosts, really, haunting the ruins.
How often we moved! How did we
ever manage to lug along with us
so much hope, abandonment, loss
and lostness? But the journeys etched
in us were all dim dreams. Not one
of our plans ever came to anything:
the keys, we supposed, to locks
that never were. Yes, on a chest,
we thought. Really! And still
it's there waiting, keyless, buried
for years like a mystery corpse. We
mustn't open the lid of a legend
like that. Everyone's life should
contain things longed-for and forgotten —
things, signs, and words —
that must be looked for in different boxes.

CE-SSE

GRAY ATTITUDES

"We can't know, can we," he used to say in those
last years, "if a swallow really can predict
a storm." The secret meanings he would hunt
down in a word, below the fragile scab
of cynicism the deep wound, death
announcing itself in the resonant voice
that had commanded a lifetime's attention.
He couldn't stand anybody, he was jealous
of time in fact his politeness sloughed off
when he snatched at time implacably decamping.
That spring we heard he could no longer sleep —
he knew before any of us it would be the last one.
So who was he? If we turn and look, life
is a deceptive trap: histories and cities, people's
names and dates and the gray attitudes
adopted in certain circumstances —
what's tall and straight interlocked with what
bows and scrapes: some of us, trying
to decipher him, might see it like that.

But people are indecipherable: like a rain
that gusts up and blows over
before we can get the umbrella open.

CE-SSE

PUGACHEV'S HISTORY

"My good friend." The tone is sarcastic. "However
we force ourselves, we surely cannot regard Pushkin
as a historian" — the years clearly haven't changed the crux
or the juncture of their dead-end quarrel: for the one,
act and actor are determined within the flow of Time;
interpretation rarely enters annals and archives. History:
our inescapable higher memory.

                                      "Chronos!"
says the other, deliberately irking his opponent.
"You can't go back and forth on time's lanes, they're twisted
like a ball of yarn: hour, day, season: these banal horizontal
and vertical axes you invent make me smile: or does Life,
good sir, stand outside your History with its own logic,
like a crossword puzzle?"

                                At midnight the women, weary,
retreat to the far end of the room and speak in low voices
of bracelets and earrings, waiting outside a cul-de-sac
that's been assayed who knows how often. Yahya Kemal's
and Cavafy's names get dropped as usual
and both men find unacceptable, for different reasons,
Pound's and Eliot's views on time and history. Traversing
"the 1509 earthquake," the poet raises his voice —
and while they know the men haven't lost their tempers
in years, the women stop talking and prick their ears

a moment like cats at a new noise, eyes glowing
with mock anxiety. Then the classic quarrels about fiction:
old findings and extraordinary new evidence meet
in the dissection of Kemal Tahir, Solzhenitsyn,
Georges Duby. Unable to bear the roosterish truculence
in the serious children's faces of these two un-
invited mattress-fluffers, the women smile and cluck
at the far end of the room.

      Toward morning the old
actor's eyelids grow heavy; he mounts a final effort
to topple Pushkin's sublimated idealism. No use:
the poet's ruthless passion for paradox propels him
to his feet. Ignoring his antagonist slouched on the sofa,
he vigorously exerts his right to extremism:
"That he was a n'er-do-well, even a bum, I understand,
I'm not blind of course. But if everyone went on
living decorously, poetry would never overthrow
the primitive rules that bedeck time. Why, after all,
should the discord, the mutiny, the heroic absurdities
that subvert progress be less important
than your Treaty of Versailles?"

Day breaks.
As if wanting to cleanse the place of talk,
the young actor gets up and puts on some music
and leans his head against the windowpane:

two women are hurrying to catch the bus, talking
to each other and looking at a holy fool lying
on a spread-out newspaper.

CE-SSE

STAYING BEHIND

Anise, fluoride, caffeine: the taste of poison
on the tongue, the sly headache, the fog clawing
at his vision — they'd done a lot to fill
the gap between night and morning. He'd stopped
shaving every day, he picked up the paper
slipped beneath his door each morning
and tossed it on the pile without a glance,
he was careless about washing the dishes,
he never ironed the shirts he wore. For the boy
waiting just beyond the door slightly ajar
he composed a creaky sentence or two:
he'd quickly dropped from daily use the verbs
he was tired of, but he kept the adjectives:
deaf and wary since being left on his own,
the phone disconnected, he never opened
the door however the bell implored, he
never went out to sit on the back balcony:
the question, were it asked, would be more
than he could bear.

CE-SSE

THE PHOTOGRAPH

He met the girl in Saloniki, fall of 1919.
I ran across a story like it once in De Quincey:
Ann of Oxford Street, he called the woman.
They met, he claimed, on a London street — and there
in broad daylight he lost, first, himself and then —
can you believe it? — all trace of her. For months
he looked for her constantly, everywhere,
but the day came (apparently even for a fanatic
like De Quincey hope and the quest have limits)
when he accepted the fact that Ann was gone —
though it's hard to say if she was truth or fiction,
especially if we remember that as an opium-eater
he could compete with Coleridge. . .

                                        His poems
all date from those years: 1919 to '34. In French,
mostly. Those years he wore his traveling shoes
to Berlin and Marseilles, like a child of Parnassus
acquainted with Prufrock — perhaps influenced
by Laforgue, perhaps inspired by "Spleen" —
but never mind, in '35 he came back here,
sixteen years, that is, after the girl had died.
He moved in with an aunt in Feriköy. I was
always curious: can one have a second life
with one's childhood friends?

What was I saying?
Oh yes, Madame Çolakyan remembers well
how he was back then: a mild-mannered man,
agreeable certainly, in the evenings they'd sit
and listen to scratchy '78s and croon along
with Maurice Chevalier and Charles Trenet.
It was standing in a silver Art Deco frame then.

Nobody around here knows him any more.
Everything we heard about what happened
just before they rushed him to the hospital
I put down as pure rumor. A terrifying
and beautiful story. There's a poem like it
in *The North Ship*: a fortune-teller tells
a sailor: you'll see: you knew the mystery girl
who came and kissed you when she died
twenty years ago by another name. If only
he could talk, even raving in his sleep, I'd sit
by his side and try to catch the searing words.
I never wondered if it was a metaphor,
an idea, an invention, or the very same face
he saw: I slipped it out of his files,
I've had it ever since.

CE-SSE

GLORIA

"The root of the problem, I think, is that we've lost
Cicero's *Gloria* — anyway, Petrarch read it before
he wrote that pompous *Epistola*." The old poet gets up
and for the umpteenth time opens the window to air
the low-ceilinged room choked with cigarette smoke.
The other slowly perks up: by his manner you can tell
he's of an age that still believes the night is not bottomless:
"The *Vita di Dante* puts it perfectly: the guy's a fool for fame obviously,
don't be taken in by the *Purgatorio's* clever posing,
he blurts it out — *grido, rumore, nominanza, onore* — he's
trying to say these words are empty, but deep inside
he thrills to the thought of wearing the crown."
And so the tempest passes. The old poet feels relieved,
those letters dashed off in Barcelona to a prospective translator,
that bit of lobbying before the prize, dissolve like mist.
They're quiet a while. All at once between them there's a feeling,
as if behind the door were someone who could hear.

CE-SSE

BALCONY

"Sweetheart, my darling, my Héloise, come
to me, jump in my lap." Sweet-talking guy,
in his voice that odd soft tone
we keep for newborn babies: "What nonsense
wasn't it for me to give you a name like that,
what nonsense wasn't it?" He laughed
from deep down and went on silently:
What nonsense Héloise and Abélard, History
and Time, what nonsense Life and Death,
cats and words and poems.

And Héloise? Long gone to the balcony:
in a huge ink bottle spilled on the sky
whirling from evening to night
she was madly chasing her tail.

CE-SSE

THE HIGH PASTURES

Four days after the coup, precisely, they found it possible
to hold commencement exercises: my friends
didn't leave me alone for a minute, even Sister Marie,
with whom I'd fought for years, came to me
and warily brushed my hair. There wasn't a girl
who didn't cry. Yet the only one who stayed stuck
to her chair, frozen, lifeless, when her name was read out,
was I: who was it in me that went up to the principal,
who held in her hand the red-ribboned diploma,
then like a sleepwalker crossed the quadrangle
and vanished into the building? I still
don't remember what idea drove the logic
of those scenes: I could only go to Yassıada once,
since that day it's never been off my mind,
the image of that scarecrow sitting on the stool
my uncle showed me — not that, nor the heat wave,
nor the coffin at Teşvikiye Mosque, nor my mother's
choice of total silence: life, a seal.

They say this summer's the hottest ever in Istanbul.
Each night I lie down on the balcony with my lover
and listen to Reggiani deep in the dark, grief
undiminished. He'll be twenty-six this week,
he's a private bank guard. I love the way

he looks around the parlor with child-like wonder:
as his eyes roam over the Yıldız vases, the crystal fire
of Murano chandeliers, the Wedgewood ashtray
where he shyly taps his cigarette, perhaps he's thinking
of his childhood and the black tents on the high pastures
he told me about one morning when he woke up —
his fingers toying with a keepsake from my father:
an agate seal.

                            CE-SSE

C.

A journal entry, Torino, 3 March 1946.
At that point he hadn't yet met the woman —
this woman who was an eternal spring of coolness
in the sticky Roman heat and, he clearly believed,
an amphora of unsoundable depth. But he ran
and managed to cross to the far side of the sea
where, etched in invisible ink, the big question mark
crooked its finger. Now, rotten cheese. Pockmarked flesh.
Cold trail of light long gone from the eye.
Her hands are shaking, who knows how many drinks
this one makes? Whisky and beauty married
in a long metastasis: the boat is weighing anchor
on its own. "Okay, but why, Constance?" I ask.
She says, "I don't remember anyone by that name."
The angel of goodness to whom she's tuned her soul:
Deception. New Jersey 1989: summer's last breath,
in time's dead center the heavy plumb-bob.

CE-SSE

PASSPORT

Aunt Aagoni died in '78, after that life was hard

for my great-uncle, being alone is tough for an old man,

I went to see him first thing the year I started law school,

my mother sent dates and a sweater — he lived in a single room,

I can see it in my mind, that house on Tomtom Street, not untidy

exactly, still it seemed a part of the boundless promise

of the vagabond life, as if he were always ready to head out

to a far-off place he was already late in leaving for.

Passport.

162938

KINGDOM OF EGYPT

No. of Passport	36424
Name of Bearer	Armenag Shaheniantz
National status	Egyptian Subject
Profession	Sales Manager
Place and date of birth	Baghdad, 1904
Domicile	Cairo
Height	171 cms.
Color of eyes	Brown
Color of Hair	Black
Countries for which this Passport is valid	Palestine

The Validity of this Passport expires   4th January 1934
    unless renewed.

Issued at Cairo
Date 5.1.1933

I tried talking to him of course but you know how after a certain age
people's ideas get all mixed up: what they think at any one time
gets tangled with a chunk of the past and in an order whose logic
they alone grasp, words, images and a symbol or two spill out
one after the other. He was somewhat preoccupied by Eastman's
suicide — in '32 he'd just started working for Kodak in Beirut
when they got the news, and he still couldn't understand why
an old man would give up life just like that. Then again he'd harp
on his arriving in Istanbul on December 9, 1936, that date
was like a talisman in his long migration — he didn't come here,
actually, to settle for good: Farouk's succession to the throne,
everything in the Middle East was confused in those years:
the Peel Report, executions, Jews and Arabs rebelling and dying
by the hundreds, plus it seems quite a few British, Hitler's gift
of the Mercedes, Kodak's management full of indecision:
he didn't belong here, my great-uncle: the passport in your hand
shows it: he couldn't manage to make his wandering body settle:
not in Baghdad where he was born, not in Cairo where he'd fetched up,
not in Beirut, not even in Istanbul where he froze into stillness:
he fell to earth like an alien, and like an alien he picked up and left.

[34]

In 1908 Freud published a short essay, on the surface as plain as unbuttered toast, called "Poetic Creativity and Day-dreaming," where for the first time he juxtaposes the child and the poet in the expression of fantasy: a certain energy potential which the ordinary man silences or suppresses breaks through and displays itself when children play or a poet writes or a neurotic talks: as for other people, they're jammed up and locked tight.

"How is it," says Freud, "that the poet can grasp and put into words those sensations and emotions which the rest of us, if we encountered them, couldn't hope even to recognize, let alone express?" Toward the end of the essay he'll come close to the key: "The technique that in essence embodies the *ars poetica* consists in overcoming that feeling of repression in us which is connected, without doubt, with the barriers and relationships that arise between every *I* and every other *I*; the real mystery is there."

With the first pieces, the major anxiety that rose up developed paradoxically into the major impetus as I went along: I really did have a stock of experience I could trust to some degree to help me in moving from a poetics with a high degree of abstraction to a poetics with a high degree of narration: on a line that runs from "The Tropic of Scorpio" through "Fugue" I'd used both narrative techniques and "theatrical" devices. Still, here and there the poems of *The Gray Divan* continued to raise certain problems of equilibrium between narrative and dramatic elements that made me squirm — so long as the floating fantasy period that Freud described in that essay (absolutely accurately in my opinion) was being enriched by relationships of revelation (mentioned in the same text) between the *I* and the other *I's*, the process was becoming on the one hand more and more complex; on the other hand it was that very process which was bringing out the poem!

[35]

If only that floating time-curve that breaks out of its focus in the here and now to fluctuate back and forth between a point in the past (childhood) and an indeterminate but desirable point in the future could have been limited to the *I* writing the poem! But the person(s) who comprise the poems' subjects exhibited with their *I*'s a different curve of possibilities; and moreover, *I-I* was not always the subject of the poem. At whatever point I situated myself, however — and in one or two instances beyond — it was still *I* who was writing the poem: my fantasies, together with those that I loaded onto the other *I*'s, or sometimes extracted from them, became paths of the same labyrinth as far as the book as a whole was concerned.

Can it be said that *The Gray Dîvan*, from one end to the other, with all its varied sequencing, enacts a novelistic structure?

They emptied the bedroom bureau's bottom drawer and gave
the contents to Vahan Bey: a stack of letters wrapped in plastic
and tied with a rubber band, an account book full of — now —
meaningless sums, a passport, a Chamber of Commerce file.
I know it, that house on Tomtom Street: just below the Spaniards,
adjacent to the garden, a two-storey ruin: the front faces
the old Palace of Justice, on one side is the Italian Consulate —
the registers of depth here are different, it's a weird dark lake
for me: if I go down that street, when I pass a certain point
light flashes from a small church bell: though still
I have no prayer, nor place nor tongue to pray it in,
slowly, with an alien sorrow, I descend, how could I
have known he lived there, or if I had known, what difference
would it have made? — Vahan Bey has spread the bank flyers

[36]

on the table, a few old movie posters next to a spray

of pictures illustrating a series in *Le Juif Errant* catch

the eye, the antique civil servant is discussing gravely

with a friend the fine points of Bozcaada wines, a safety pin

fixes his coin purse to his coat, his short-haired large-faced cat

refuses to budge from his feet, I reach out and take the passport.

CE-SSE

GYPSY TENTS

I

There's a nook fixed in the front of the tent
farthest back: it's where the chief always sits,
his guest, if he's got one, beside him. Where
we're sitting. "Keskin," they call him. "Sharp."
A razor's maybe hidden in his gaze. "You're good
at word-slinging," he says. "Everyone admires it,
everyone's scared of it." I explain how city folk
flee rhetoric like a scarecrow: why the crowd's
always average and dull. Behind his eyes lurks
a swarm of tricks: questions, hints; then a gleam
of teeth in the dark: streak of light in the sky.
"To pry is a shameful thing." He shrugs, quickly
sheathing his head in the night.

II

Next evening I'm shivering. He calls the girl,
has her bring a wool sweater. The girl: fifteen,
more or less. Her name: "Akik." She looks
me up and down, nakedly, black eyes glowing
with a scorpion's defiance. He's not blind.
"Go on," he says. "Quit hanging around

the gentleman." She goes a little way off
to collect some twigs and sticks, I light
a cigarette from the one I'm smoking:
excited bellows fanning the purple sky.
"That one's blood is wild: wherever we go,
she's trouble. Here everyone pulls his own weight,
but she's the one Keskin keeps an eye on."
She brings the sticks she's gathered and
feeds them one by one into the fire. Out of
the corner of my eye I observe her hair,
her wrist, her breast rising and falling.
"Hey now," says the chief, "I said don't
be hanging around."

III

On the last night they break out the *rakı* —
drums, *zurna*, the fine melancholy of violins.
No gambling, no joking, no dancing boys,
silently and solemnly men drink with men.
The noise of the city slowly settles, only
the weary growling of a stream of trucks
punctuates the music. I rise and wander
toward the hill: deep in the heart of the night
the beguiling hint of a shadow is beckoning.
I'm calling softly, a sally against the void —

They've got a mirror in the jail

Hey girl, there's a tattoo on your arm.

On my shoulder, suddenly, the touch of Keskin's hand.

CE-SSE

PHTONOS

"It's said that in Ancient Greece some gods had no body.
What held them was not a figure but a sound, a sign."
He tossed back his silver hair behind his ears,
resting between his sentences:
"Which always reminds me of Mozart's Requiem:
if a hand helps, death and life can survive
in the same pot of plants. If one feeds off the other,
which is it, I wonder? Some questions we can't answer
seep through the years, pool in our life." Distraction.
Recalling a rainy Salzburg morning, perhaps
his memory is overrun by images of the hospital
where he was taken, following the night he began
the last movement of his first violin concerto.
"Behind the chorus cowers fear itself, solitary,
insurmountable: choosing which way to turn at crossroads
appears the most chilling of decisions to me
— he smiles ruefully for an instant — perhaps that's why
I could never step over the threshold I reached."

Hard seed, fertile soil — if watered separately,
could also feed each other: roots mix, an impossible tangle,
a heavy snarl weaves through shared survival.
But if it's really true that some gods live without body,
then the sound ϕ settles in a dark spot in the room:

the pot cracks, the soil dries up, so many deaths

can pitch their pavilion in our life as we live on.

SP

IN THE MIRROR

Burlington socks, Edinburgh porcelain for
that first cup of morning tea, a special pleasure
taken in the piano so early in the morning,
those years when I was picky about everything.
Glory and vanity, a cynicism behind which
I tried to suppress the curl of a sneering lip:
the force of that worn-out mask of mockery
as I wove my way through the elitist conceits
of the middle and upper classes in style, like
a slalom skier! Now my chauffeur is washing
the Bentley's windows, when my poems
were published in Buenos Aires and Udine
my publisher said, "I knew it was your turn this year
for the *Prix Internationale des Critiques*" —
advertising consultant for a big spaghetti firm,
member and advisor of the editorial board
who arrives at morning meetings with notes
scribbled down the night before, a mentor
whom the liberals phone for advice before
budget debates: Burlington socks, underwear
from the PX, cheese from Denmark — they all
help my breakfast hour speed quickly by.

My second wife died last year, my eldest son's
an ambassador in Oslo, the middle one chose
to stay and rot at the university, only the last
one is like me, a bit rakish: for his last lover
he tried to write a *dîvan* in Persian. If I have
no close friends, neither do I have enemies.
That minor scandal with the young actress
is forgotten, the odd reaction I displayed
in the face of the inheritance suit is lost
to memory. The Senate ought to be
re-established. I should, like Montale,
be granted the right for life to address it.
Half a century I've been a poet: I lived my life
with this country's forgotten, forgetful words,
while you shouldered past that selfsame life: *you.*

CE-SSE

SUNDAY BOREDOM

At Çukurcuma a feast of hats: tulle and veil,
one left from Nowotny nights,
the other from the first Democrat Party ball:
between Armistice and Democracy
a jumbled museum.

At Topkapı a bundle of rags: birthplace Vienna,
citizenship Austro-Hungarian Empire,
year on year in Tarlabaşı
flew the broker's iron coop —
stocks, bonds, title deeds,
the Kaiser's big banknotes.

At Üsküdar a sad treasury of bric-á-brac:
mother-of-pearl buttons, console radio
innards, souvenir brass ashtray
from a Florida hotel, whose
glasses are these, whose hours
in the amber beads
thumbed by a patient hand
have sputtered out at last?

And *Never on Sunday* — videotape
with tattered label waiting
beside a watch chain,
hopeless.

CE-SSE

THE WAITING

Who did you say was hell?
I too saw the birds of sadness
flying forth and back from the tip of the flute,
yes I know, everything is a thing
of my own thinking, these words are, how can one say,
like so: just as you're about to catch them . . .

We were out for a walk in the rain that day,
I never forget details, who it was
of course I don't remember, how important
can names be, yes, I can't get the face
into focus either, it was September, a September,
who was it you were saying was hell?

CE-SSE

IN THE DESERT

In Fact

"Before you, it seems, were two roads.
On one of them you got scared, I see,
and before long turned back. The other one —
the familiar one you'd set foot on and forsaken
several times — you supposed would be safe.
Now it's petered out. You can't keep going
on this one, and you've lost your way
to that one: here's your endless narrow
labyrinth; there's the wall you're up against.
Oh, and that road you were so afraid of
turns out in fact to be the horizon."

If Only

"You're shut up in the cup you turned over.
In all my years as a witch, I've rarely seen
a self-forged fate like this. If I told you,
'Get up and come out,' you couldn't move.
And if you stay there . . . nobody's ever managed
to live in the dark he's cut out for himself.

In the boundless space within me I see a room

for you: you'll pace it every night —

if only there were an exit."

As If

"I saw hands: hedged, nervous, fiery lines

I took in my hand —

one I can't forget belonged to you,

another to the man with the scattered look

I met when I was young: between you

caravans come and go nonstop,

somebody's always packing big suitcases,

migratory birds, flighty gazelle,

tell me, have you been marked, a sacrifice,

or have you been spared, sad-eyed angel? —

it's as if, like a dead weight before you both,

stood time."

CE-SSE

"MIGRATORY BIRD"

I

Alone and wounded, like an enormous bird
he appeared to Hamdi Bey: in his room
he listened to the hotel's bowels murmuring
every evening: who knew how many winters
lay curled behind the summers, sleep had long ago
abandoned him. He didn't remember the sunshine
now, or the women he'd wrapped in mist,
even the stations were ground to bits in the teeth
of a famished tunnel rat gnawing its own era.
A windowpane from the house where he was born,
a back street in Montparnasse, a pine tree
in Beylerbeyi, the rough bark warming his palm,
an insidious rain whose where or when
he couldn't fathom: wandering the tip of his tongue
in halting rhythm, an unfinished line —
his life.

II

His eyelids were as weary as the memory
endlessly sifting images from a great bank
of snowy silence like a notebook in the wind

flipping to the same pages again and again.
In the photograph that began to yellow
the day it was snapped in Warsaw, his long-
vanished staff still tricked out the embassy's
thick boredom with the snap and crack
of firewood stacked against undying winter.
They never ceased to taste of defeat,
those words that he'd pulled together
out of a tangle of high-flown feelings —
"Suddenly to fall into the desert /
and yearn like a soul burning with thirst"—
between two lines an absolute blank
when he kept them to himself,
he never knew why.
                    Next morning
he walked out never to return. The season
lay like an overcoat on his back
fear froze his face
locked to its perch inside him
a restless sparrow hawk whistled an unknown tune.
Suddenly his eyes flew open: from that moment
to this that first encounter had haunted his mind,
in his ears Friday's footprint
howling.

III

The nurse fluffs the pillow under his head.

Later this evening Sermet Sami might drop by,

a phone call could come from Ankara,

or a cool breeze from Erenköy just for him.

"Oh God, don't leave me like this!

This grief in my heart has worn me out."

Time's a chain of misunderstandings: no one

lives things in the correct order: now

like a perpetually spinning top Münir

goes waltzing by, and that sticky summer

in Biarritz, the sage tea sipped at Çengelköy,

the arbor at Martinho da Arcada

where he sat in the shady quiet and drank

nonstop for days on end. The nurse smoothly

shuts the door. The sun won't rise in the same spot

again, it won't set again in the same spot,

that ship of seamless silence.

CE-SSE

FUGUE XVII

"Well then, when will the book be finished?"

"So," she's asking, "Where and when, really, do you begin
your book?" "Hard to say," says the poet. "I think it's
clear only later: poetry's like a progressive disease —
usually well advanced by the time you diagnose it."
For months the book's been building in his mind while
life is put on hold: the contents of his imagination —
faces, cross-sections, hallucinations — leave their places
and re-appear in rough creations of letters and blanks.
"The words I gave up on" — smiling all at the same time
they reach the decision to retain their long silence.
"You weigh what surfaces, you poke it, probe it, pore over it
a long time; but what you wind up with is only the grating
residue of the poem that's skated through your fingers."

Nobody would know how many days he wandered the narrow
street beside the French Hospital, how those impressions etched
upon his retina so precisely when he peered behind the
curtains choked the words rising up with his rising dread:
Life, Death, Memory, Oblivion — what piled up between these
headings punctured the daily expanding bubble of his own
gloom. Nobody would know why that long poem built on
Browning stumbled, or why he laid aside the bit between

Anton and Olga that he'd grabbed and been burned by,
or how the acrostic poem he was assembling and dis-
assembling — his "Symphonie Fantastique" — vaporized
like frost on a windowpane. "Maybe all the seedlings
that failed to sprout that season could go into an Ash Dîvan:
the bittersweet History of Inventors could stand beside
The Dîvan Literature Museum which I imagined
in *nihavent* mode. Then there's 'Lady Sings the Blues' —
its bouncy meter made me tear it up —
and 'Dead Man's Poem': that one I hid out of fear.
Every book has its dark matter — a wall of stones
hard-won, left out, left over, and left unused.
Nobody would know, not even me, when that blind clock,
wound by another hand and always late, is set to strike."

"Okay, then when, exactly, is your book finished? Or is it
trying to decide whether to go on or to give up
that's choking you?" She considers her question, aware
that some answers must follow an uncivilized silence.
"If you're asking when a book is *really* finished, that's something
the poet himself may not know until well after it's published:
one day the light might flare briefly up from a single poem
like a thunderclap that cracks across the evening sky
long after the lightning flash. But even then he might not get it."

[54]

The closer he comes to nailing the book together,
the harder it is to sleep. Some nights he'll lie down
an hour or two, then leap up again. A solitary light
glows in a far-off window, a bunch of rags spill
from a garbage can and sail away, a plane, light blinking
in the dark sky, flies who knows from where to where.
Some nights he sits at his desk and fiddles with the short-wave,
some nights he returns to bed without going near his desk.
There are mornings when he wakes up brim-full. Nights
when he's all dried up. He goes for a walk, chasing the solution
just beyond his reach. Like a gamin dancing on the tip
of his tongue, the tune flees at the moment he closes in.
At this point a wish-ribbon, a taste of magic, a talisman —
these are what he's searching for.

CE-SSE

QUARANTINE

I'm tired, Enis, of always being me, and the others in me. "I'm locking myself in my room," I once said, "when I set sail on the open sea." Like an enormous stomach the water undulated and puked up my cabin: that's where I lived out, one after the other, first a melancholy exuberance and then the full spectrum from horror to enlightenment, see-sawing between madness and stoic patience. Traversing coal-black desert, ice-blue sky and my silkworm dreams, I dropped anchor here. "Wait," said a voice, stern and even, but hurt. "We'll measure the contagion in you: Who knows, you might come this way again, or be a carrier from one harbor to the next."

If I turned and looked back, who knows how many hundreds of fathoms deep lie, waiting for me, the shipwrecks I deserted: a chest full of gold coins, treaties between ocean empires with seals and signatures still warm, a ruby ring and silver cathedral candelabra, delicate glassware blown in the East and bronze hammered out in the West — one by one, in the depths of the open sea, I abandoned every ship I ever boarded. I chased my life and ran away as soon as I caught it: I'm a secret cowardly pirate without an earring: from night to night the only prize I take is the infernal treasure in which I'm buried.

CE-SSE

FROM MARSEILLES, THE END

for Orhan Koçak

Dear Teddie, a proper life
can however be lived erroneously —
I throw the dice in my hand:
the speed and angle I give them,
the surface they'll strike, the length of their fall
I adjust, if from my brain
and the tips of my nerves and muscles
the calculation shoots out . . .

There's your face: solid, withdrawn,
like a thermostatic mask: by the time
you read these lines I'll be long gone.
"My friend," said the fortune-teller I met last night,
"Unpack your suitcase, take off your coat:
whether you go or stay in fact is all the same:
your death was lost the day before the day
you reached the threshold of the endless sea."

CE-SSE

[57]

PHANTOM PAIN

"Wiener Magdeberg took this photograph,"
Aunt Semiha had said, "in the Ayaspaşa mansion."
Light-colored eyes pierce out of a darkened face.
He was in the fourth front at Anafartalar
when a cannonball burst a few meters behind him.
Talat Pasha himself had him transported to Tübingen,
to the military hospital where they cut off his right leg
a span above the knee. He remained there a year,
writing three or four times a week that he was in good health,
filling up the backs of postcards with a neat hand.
Once his wound had healed they spared no expense,
had a prosthesis made for him, each day trained him to walk,
offered psychotherapy. It was during the Armistice
that he at last sailed from Hamburg to Istanbul.

My aunt sensed, as they embraced at Karaköy,
the real wound that ran inside him ceaselessly.
Then winter came and brought the grievous aching
that some French doctor had named phantom pain.
It was on the morning of March 17, 1920,
from the little pier in Kalender, that he rowed out.
"Every night," had said Aunt Semiha, "I wake up,
feel the empty side of the bed with my hand,
and think, at first, 'He's sleepless again.'

[58]

All that keeps me connected to life is this fixation
that lasts a few seconds each day."

SP-MK

AT SÂDÎ'S GRAVESIDE

Each time I shut my eyes and turn to face mild spring sunlight, I see a woman waiting at Sâdî's grave in Shiraz. There's a face, its features erased, only her long black hair spiraling out across the curtain of my eyes. Behind the grave, far off, a horseman waits for the woman. The horse's harness hangs loose, can it be a single ray of sunlight flashing from the stirrup that deludes me, I can't tell, as I hold out my hand to touch the woman's hair, it bursts into flames, the sun suddenly eclipsed. Then I'm walking towards the well just beside the grave, you'd think I'm in a dream, dreaming. The well is deep, the source of the water unclear, evidently it's inhabited by sacred bird-fish, nobody knows their origins, whoever approaches them dies at once, yet I —

SP-MK

PULSE

"I'm death's lieutenant," he was saying
in the letter mailed afterward, the U.N.
conference of 25 February produced
Security Council Resolution No. 1451,
on the basis of which the battalion
sent as a symbolic gesture to the region
six days earlier was to occupy the buffer zone
just outside the city, his helmet tightly fastened
between ear and neck a warm ache —
in the artillery barrage triggered by so
decisive a finger no one could really know
for sure if it were a stray bullet that pierced
the absolute silence at the bottom of his mind
before the wine's blood came from his nose
and throat and spread across his chest,
looking for a pulse, "My lieutenant is dead,"
says the child-faced soldier.

CE-SSE

SIEGE OF THE JACKALS

When he said I gave up my pen and took up the gun
René Char was right; you have to give up the pen
before you take up the gun I believe:
on the one hand write and on the other puke,
this split is intolerable to our being
I who was always torn in two was saying,
writing with one hand and erasing with the other,
writing with one hand and writing with the other,
from any angle still I was whole —
now these, it's clear, are most difficult times:
between grasping the one and dropping the other
my hand wavers: in front of me a bridge
I don't want to cross, inside me a fire
I don't want to keep burning, outside
the jackals, quiet, ready.

CE-SSE

CONVERSING WITH ATTAR

[740-746; 4869-4901]

My poetry, my *dîvan*,

you were saying it brims with ravings,

slowly I descended time's steep steps,

call out to me, I begged, give me a voice,

just one sound to start, I said

and listened:

let a feather from your wing

fall on this land,

let the fine imagery you've woven so gently

fly off to other lands,

you said,

a feather that will stir cities

to touch one another,

to pick the secret lock linking sound to sound,

to shed all the prattle masked as sense,

you can keep your mystery

but don't ever let it remain with you,

beware from now on

of the picture you've drawn.

Scent of blood, you'd said,

your tired face calm,

here, the last sound you gave me,

the final key,

ultimate fearlessness;

I spoke and gained nothing, true;

I kept quiet

and stashed away all I'd won

for another sun, another night, true:

the feather that blew off me

whirling down the steep steps I climbed slowly.

Cities will all lie in ruins,

my letters will be erased,

the engravings of my face on stone tablets, shattered,

the sheets of my raving *dîvan*

left black, shrivelled, unreadable,

in void already I

am all ash.

SP-MK

TREASURE

"Treasure is like glass," says Cyrus. "It glitters,
but it shatters." If I write on glass or a mirror,
it goes to pieces. If I write on wood or paper,
it goes up in flames. I wrote on stone:
the wind's shrewish tongue wiped it off.
My poetry, my treasure: If I write on the sun,
one day it will set, if I write on the night,
the period, the comma, the question mark
will be up in the stars. Darkness like glass
glitters and shatters, says a dark voice in me —
one thing alone remains: a hush: my petrified alphabet.

CE-SSE

THE CURTAIN

Both sides of the sea, actually, are boiling
with legends: regarding things known,
we are the knowing subjects, yet the objects
have long since risen to the plane of
the unknown: the manuscripts are lost,
not a stone remains of those great cities
we could have gone to see. As for people,
well, are they fact or fiction? No one's left
to confirm the reality of events we once
believed in — take the dubious stories about
those Theseus paintings by the Corinthian,
Euphranor, and Parrhasios of Ephesus:
Euphranor said, supposedly, "His Theseus
was fed on roses, mine on plain meat."
Not a square centimeter of either painting
has come down to us. They say he composed
a treatise on colors and ratios, vanished now
into thin air, like those marble sculptures,
each one more wonderful than the last, gone
without a trace: would time, pulverizer
of granite, hold back for mere papyrus?

Anyway a legend is like a beautiful woman,
how can it be true always and everywhere?

Those imaginary faces, sieved by time
offer a taste of the real that somewhat jars
with the truth. For all we know, what we find
in the archives might have been concocted
in Athens: the grapes in Zeuxis' painting looked
so real, the birds tried to peck them. And as they
came flying, so we go flying to that day:
now came the Ephesian's turn; the young painter
threw down the gauntlet: "Open the curtain
hiding your painting, and let's see who's come
closer to reality." Just here, I think, is where
we encounter true genius: although we've lost
the original, its secret leaps down to us through
the centuries: it's the curtain itself — yes!
that turns out to be the painting.

CE-SSE

FOR TITIVILLUS

Whenever I see copyists in a figurative painting
from antiquity — are there any non-figurative
ones? — or illuminations of monkish life
on a medieval manuscript, I move in closer.
Is he visible? Invisible Titivillus,
to them too he never showed himself,
apparently, though he had a sack on his back,
a sack to hold the syllables the bored monks
forgot to copy. Each misspelling meant a tick
in his notebook; but can anyone not space out
or get carried away if he's making a fair copy
of a monograph by Iamblichus or an obscene poem
by Sybaris? One by one he would reckon up
such sins to await the Day of Judgment.

I've never seen him or heard his voice, but
when I'm writing sometimes I feel his presence.
Wherever I turn my back that's where he is,
I know, or at least guess: from the get-go
his fingers seem to twitch with each mistake
I make, as with great glee he jumps on reasons
to send me to hell. But to hew to the right,
we need the wrong; as for those who judge
other people right or wrong . . . doesn't he get it

yet, that damned *djinn*, that senile angel
who long ago retired into oblivion?
I swear he ought to roast in hell himself:
how, if I hadn't written this poem,
would anyone know he'd ever existed, even,
let alone done his meddlesome work?
But hey, he's a legend: so come on then,
what the hell, let's go together, hand in hand.

CE-SSE

DIGENIS

The colored stones are set side by side,
postage stamps, with the logic of beads
that spiral in prayer and echo like a pulse
sent through to the fingers' juncture: from end
to end, borders, black, scarlet, purple-blue,
mold-green, enclose a hopscotch harmony
worked from odd-shaped chips of bone-white,
gray, mud-yellow stone; as we look up,
in any corner, a voice of color, full of words:
angel, last judgment, a kneeling figure
and those made pure, form, stone by stone,
in the swift traversing gaze. None can
know the loss that would remain, silent
in the plastered ground, should, one by one, they fall:
. . . *Once out of nature I shall never take*
My bodily form from any natural thing,
But such a form as Grecian goldsmiths make
Of hammered gold and gold enamelling
To keep a drowsy Emperor awake — did
he think so when he first came in? I try
to visualize him when he disembarked
on the quay in Istanbul — he must have come
by sea — *The Tower*, the first edition,
1928, he bought in an Oxford

bookshop should have been in his hand — like
the Englishmen he admired, sometimes using
his umbrella as a walking stick, and the way
he made an effort to be taken for
a young man: *That is no country for old men.*
I try to visualize him leaning
against the garden wall of the timbered house
on Caferiye Street; he looks a long time
at the cloud-stopping dome and then walks,
his steps unsteady, toward the door.
Come from the holy, a voice within him
says, startling him, and he knows then that
Time, reaching back and forward, is full
of endless knots, stretching, to become a rope.
And when he does go in, he seems to hear, distinct,
the silence prepared for him through many centuries.
Bending to the stone he reaches out, touches
cold Phrygian marble, caresses it, lifts
his head, draws into his lungs that special smell
spreading in the air. Scarcely discernible,
the Stone is moving. So it seems to him.
The light of morning, ascending step by step,
touches the vaults and as he comes to the exact
center of the floor, a deep voice, booming
like a psalm, descends resounding from the walls
and ringing in his ears; echoes beyond

number, cluster-like cells dividing

beneath the dome, spreading, and, for an instant,

at the most gathered point of both sound

and light, meeting, and then, sundering,

as with the blood pumping to the brain,

the momentary vertiginous stop.

And then: as though countless murmuring voices

are brought to birth, atoms from the whirling

cries, he stands, as if ice, dumbstruck by the place.

In terror he searches for the great angel's deep

and somber face as it seems about to spill

from the narthex's plastered front.

Before me floats an image, man or shade,

Shade more than man, more image than a shade.

I try to visualize him, a slim, tall

silhouette, his mass of hair, long since gone gray,

making his face seem small, his habit

of settling his glasses with a finger,

and the apartment flat he rented at Taksim,

spread with all those tracings, sketches, drawings.

And dawn chasing figures who appear

and disappear in the streets he enters

and the run-down coffeehouse he would go down to

beside the Golden Horn — that's where he meets

Arif and Abidin. The icons, their

tensed faces massed, can scarcely be seen

in the haze of smoke. The hashish crackles
in the hubble-bubble. On the backs
of matchboxes, his huge shadow bent low,
Arif, his pencil scrupulously sharp,
draws Byzantine faces. On Bible-black cards
Abidin catches the ash-white faces
of the flying junkies. In the atelier
on the Rue de l'Eure, Samih gets the camera
ready. Güzin pours more tea. Abidin drinks
lots of water, his throat is always dry. His eyes
search the past. He says, "He brought Arif and me
to Hagia Sophia like a man possessed.
Walking on the rickety wooden bench
slanting to the Emperor's Gate like apprentice
acrobats, we stopped in front of a façade black
with soot. Whittemore bent down, picked up a bucket
full of water and splashed the figure
hesitating in the dark depths of the wall.
Straightaway, bright, wet, fresh colors sprang from the void."
He said no more. All you could hear was the sound
of the camera. Samih and I go out
and walk in silence to Montparnasse. He seems
to be running and rerunning in his mind
the same scene as I am. As evening falls,
the lights of the tower, a relief of discs
glinting in the sky, chase some ancient appearance

in the memorial void. *Spirit after*
spirit! More image than a shade. It was
the year I came back to Istanbul. I bought
some documents from a secondhand bookseller,
among them papers that had belonged
to Ali Sami Boyar; his typescript of
"Western Authors of the Byzantine
and Post-Byzantine Period," with revisions
in hand; bibiographical notes he made on
the Diegesis when he was Director
of Hagia Sophia; a letter dated
27 September 1940
in response to a telephone inquiry
from Dr. Naumann saying the date of the fire
given as breaking out in 393,
in Schneider's book, was, in fact, 20 June
404; a memorandum of six notes
dated 24 June 1943, signed
"your friend and little assistant
Metropolitan Gennadios" and written
with more than obsessive care, entitled
"Answers to My Friend Ali Sami Bey's Questions"
and mailed from Arnavutköy; and four small sheets
of paper in another envelope,
daily reports jotted down in an official
hand — typewritten on the envelope

"Profösör Whittmore" and added in fountain pen,
between the second 't' and 'm' and a little
higher, an 'e'. When I tucked the sheets
of paper back in the envelope and, with
the other documents, put them in my own archive
for future reference, I had never before
heard this name. *Nine assistants worked with*
Profesör Wittemore today. Three of them
made copies on tracing paper in the semidome,
one inspected and recorded the mosaics
in the same area and two others
made freehand drawings there. Two more were
employed in cleaning the places around
the Ciharyangüzin medallions
and the architect did his own work. İhsan.
In the upper right corner of the paper
was written 29 May 1939 —
all coincidences are unnerving, all dates,
if you think about them, are like that too:
blotting out the images and sounds
I floated in, I enter upon fresh sounds,
blurred visions, scattered, fragmented in time
and space. A fearful, near silent feast
of victory must have been made in the city —
Ali Sami Bey is taking notes, from Doukas:
Why did everybody take refuge

[75]

in Hagia Sophia? Because the false prophets
had said, When the city is captured by the Turks
and the invading army comes to the Column
of Constantine, an angel will descend
and will drive the Turks into Persia as far
as the Monodendron. Whittemore leaves
the Chora together with the architect
and they walk slowly to Tekfur: talking about
Berlin, Warsaw, where the mood is increasingly
grave, and about someone they both know in London,
a city on edge; they meet, face on,
the evening, its darkened blue. At night, back in his room,
sunk deep in quite other thoughts, he shuffles
cards mechanically, the king of hearts, next to
the jack of spades, closes with the four of clubs.
A great mystery will sway upward, its edge
appearing, through the tangled script just beneath
the angel. He will fall asleep in the armchair.
From the first to the fifth of June, half the rough
cleaning of the script is finished on the vault
of the semidome where work on the mosaics
began under the direction of Mösyö (Whitemore)
this year; and the remaining part of the work
is progressing. The one photograph I have
of him must have been taken in 1931.
It's at the end of the "Primary Report

on the First Year's Work," subtitled "The Mosaics
of the Narthex," published by Oxford
University Press for the Byzantine
Institute in Paris two years later —
the first picture of that frequently
to be mentioned wheeled scaffold thirteen meters
high, with two separate floors which could be worked
on simultaneously, moving backward
and forward on rails. He had this scaffold
purposely built in Ahırkapı. I don't know
if the ones on the upper stage are
Gregorini and Benvenuti, celebrated
mosaic masters brought from Venice for this project.
I can't be sure; on the lower stage, one hand
gripping the scaffold, his head looking up,
dark suit, is that him? If, most of the time,
to know is to assume and be ready
to be deceived, then, most of the time, what is there
is true — whether I know it or nor —
especially with a photograph:
to the extent that we can see, what we see
is limited by the margin of error
in the lines of our vision, brought beyond
the level that the eye behind the camera,
and then, in all its fears, the skull hiding
behind the eye, together set and fabricate.

At that time too, there came to the city
Marangoni, responsible for the techniques
of cleaning; studying the whitewashed walls,
the photographs one by one, the plaster, deciding
how to remove it, and on the use of solvents.
Here an account in two modes, parable
and problem, takes essential shape.
Between those who cover the figures and those
who uncover them, adjusting the ways of seeing,
I too, turning and tangling, with no stop,
I cover and I clean. Faith and fear, blind
weakness, power whirl to the four compass
points. Dispersing, discriminating
the compacted cargo, I try to imagine,
seek a fifth way, a poetry toward which to turn.
Mosaic as generally known
in antiquity, says Gespach, and with its Roman,
Byzantine, and Venetian roots, is made
with small cubes attached to a solid surface
with a layer of plaster — these are either
natural stones, fired clay, or matte enamels
colored while still paste. The colored stones
are set side by side, postage stamps, with the logic
of beads that spiral in prayer and echo
like a pulse sent through to the fingers' juncture.
Out of the corner of his eye, Anthemius

saw suddenly appear on the southwest wall,
full of the harmony the quiet monk
from Cyprus sought to give it, a face.
As night ended he moved among the bodies
of the sleeping workmen and, his back
turned to the east, stood still for hours, frozen,
trying to find out how the image
would wake to the first light of day.
He crouched in the armchair, inside another's
being, dwindling through labyrinths.
Whether the calm hour hand and the brazen
minute hand are carrying the date
from the 29th to the 30th
he cannot guess. Is Justinian, pompous
before a mirror of stone, preparing
for the consecration? Or, in 754,
is the Council's last pronouncement winding up
like clockwork in his mind, in the scattered flow
of many plots? *In the name of the Trinity*
we pronounce that any icon, in whatever
material, made by the painter's burning arts,
be hurled from the Holy Church and condemned; those
who would depict images of the Second Person
of the Holy Trinity in material paints
and portraits of the saints as lifeless pictures
in material paints that have no value . . .

Wet with sweat, his mouth and palate dried up,
without moving, he sees behind the curtain
of the living room, the darkness already pierced.
A soft and misty Istanbul morning, the sparrows
welcoming summer, the dry branches of the old
linden tree in Gezi, tired already. He keeps
on dozing. Sweetly, the plumb line quivers
in his body, moving with it; deep in his eyes,
two lights contending, a pale blue backdrop shows:
Dear Henri — and so in one place and another
the years rotate, you see one age reviving
in another, it takes on glacial expanse;
look at it come closer and see: being so far
from each other, our faces prepare to turn
to ash beyond this cosmic light: everlasting
night ends day, endless night turns again to day.
The beam ricochets, refracted and scattered
into the darkness of the universe —
look at it, how color recalls itself,
Henri, how once more, once more, the form prepares
to fly, hold on to it, please, try to hold on
before the gyre, from the sky descending
and ascending, draws us all in, hold on
firm, our time is almost at an end.

CY-RT

[80]

DOOMSDAY VERSE

X, 8-9

Go, take the book held by the angel
and swallow it whole: at first
it'll leave a taste of honey in your mouth,
and within that, pangs of pain,
the letters, syllables, sentences
that, set inside you, will convulse you —
if truth enters your blood, if the seed
takes root in your organs: a truly new
core for your body, a bitter fruit,
a spiralling up, an endless rising:
this is how life melts away,
from the black-on-black horizon
that opens out gradually before you,
what lies beyond, blacker still: go,
hold to the book the angel holds.

SP-MK

ARS POETICA

They said my poetry wasn't anything special,
like Wallace Stevens's, like no one's,
maybe just "a persistence of the Second New,"
viewed possibly as "the Third New itself" —
"a batty yarn," they said, "of words and signs."
If all that sums me up, then all that I *was*.
The papers I burned, the podiums I clambered up to,
the secret cave into which I withdrew for rest
and to converse with spider, shadow, the other.
If I ever shunned or embraced myself,
that went unnoticed. The hand I thrust
into the fire, the clock onto which I locked
my gaze, the rare days when I crashed into people
bound me to a spot where sound and word
stood and stared the other down.

I was young, too young — I'd imagined
poetry as order: an ordeal of my mind,
catharsis and home, walking ever with me,
a mirror for my forsaken face, pitch-black water
splashing my body in night's spring, I imagined.

Years in the dregs sketched out another path.
No doubt I still imagine: the faith I keep

in the daybreak clearly arises from

the daredevil of deep sleep at my back.

Poetry is neither order nor chaos.

It may only be a whimsical focal point that lies

between two extremes to trip up time.

A snare, perhaps, on the threshold of rare sounds,

a question lying within the curl of a bell,

in the throat, way down at gut-point,

rolling out at my slightest movement

from a dark nook, a ball of lust,

maybe that. Not order, but —

anticipation, a clock-spring, stubborn ember,

always a phoenix.

That I started out from diamond

and set forth to glean diamond from coal,

I never forgot: if my fate was spelled out in fire,

then I'd come someday to write in fire.

Each of my letters must be a spark,

each word borne out by tongues of flame —

such a blaze that all, bleeding,

must drink their fill from the darkness

flaming within me. That

was my desire.

SP-MK

ELEGIES: THE SARCOPHAGUS OF MOURNING WOMEN

Viator, viator!
Quod tu es, ego fui; quod nunc sum, et tu eris.

— *Carmina Epigraphica*

I

If one day you should die,
that very instant on my sky
would be etched a meteor of flame,
here, in the caravan creaking from town to town,
is the tent I folded and put away,
the anticipation I kept
in a riddle pitched from day to night
at each precise oasis secretly left behind,
the water's song will not vainly trail
this drop from the spring
— unheard lyre.

II

If ever I should feel, the memory
of touch crusted over — how long! —

will stir and tremble on my skin,

a long shudder shake the clock-spring

that held its breath in a dark nook

and the panes of all the windows in me break

now one's been opened;

the hourglass I reversed and set aside

will swagger up, each grain of sand prepared

to melt in my fountain: there was a time, once,

you left this land in sorrow.

III

If like a blow the news fell, if

the stuttering of a leaden tongue

shaped that leaden sentence: in me

a silent, endless boat

quickly and softly sets sail

toward a skyline lost long ago,

dawn comes no more now, nor dusk,

nor is a place left in my breast

for nights, I hear your voice

hiding under seaweed,

solid salt cloaks me, secret.

IV

Who could say you've gone, who
could summon the courage to accost
all the meanings to crack on my face —
I don't know, anxious, I look
beside me for the strong medicine
to cure me of my five senses —
if, in the painful turn of the wheel
I thought would bear every burden,
every spoke should crack — at a stroke —
my own sap would first gush forth
from the earth for which they are preparing you.

V

I say: keep it a secret from me
that the kite has vanished from sight,
let the mirrors in the house be draped,
and my light, and the surfaces that swallow it;
if for a moment I could see my eyes
the stone in me would sweat, my light go dark,
I would see into the night beyond night
and remember the shared wind,
I would remember the town's rooftops:

keep it secret that you flew from the waters I hid —
I am a snarl of ivy tangled in my own sky.

VI

Already I see, gathered in relief, my face
on the face of the tomb, dark, a storm
massed within thunderclouds;
my body begins its long deliquescence,
autumn's habit, falling through a distance
whose two ends are forgotten,
pain settles in the lines of my face
hidden in my hand then deserts
to the seed smoldering in me.
I'll weep on the north face
of the tomb, ship with a broken rudder.

VII

You're dead it seems, in me
you'd been dead for years, I thought
I'd buried you so, unwashed,
years and years ago, before ashes gathered ash.
I'd lived with you because of you

I thought, I almost died because of you,
it was a long time, a long time before
I rose up from where I'd crumpled
and believed you were no longer living.
I'll bring my hands together on the tomb:
my face a curtain, my breast a plumb line in stone.

VIII

One day you would die I knew
the marble is hard, I could have wished
for a pair of hands at work there,
I wasn't there before, I wished for a pair of hands
to carve, hands that could be yours,
I wasn't there yet, but had been long ago.
If it hadn't happened, it would happen
one day I knew, but who first?
I hoped and prayed and lit a candle
and as it melted drop by drop before me, stood:
you were walking, silent, though dead long ago.

IX

I felt the wound aching in memory,
a stubborn rain brought on before the rain
like the one we walked through, naked
and trembling, from tree to tree,
an island we reached on any map we found.
Wild strawberry scent. Morning haze.
On earth the kneading of flesh — then
the momentous rift. Once more the gathering of clouds,
I see, a late migrant bird
looks toward the rain, flies off,
stamped on my frozen gaze — herald.

X

To me you left no grief, no anger, no grudge
I discovered; of that jealous cell that wormed
so deep into my essence, no trace:
our lives seemed to swell in crescendo,
then ebbed in the same bed. If my eyes fill with tears
it's not because you're gone: I'm left here like this,
the meaning you gave me from a distance
is where you took it — you should have waited,
if you'd just waited, we'd find our lost landmark:

I looked for it, I'll go back and look again,
it must come back, the bird I let fly away.

XI

It should face south, this carving of me.
Lost among these unhappy women
who speak neither to each other nor to death —
is that what offends me? Locked in this question,
head high, back straight, I stand and flaunt
the woman in me: only my eyes are cast down.
Let nobody think anyone else could hold me.
From now on I'll not let down my long hair,
I won't swell gently, even in season,
my lips won't burst into flower.
Carve in stone, if it's so easy, what's gone from me.

XII

Wherever I put myself I'll be on the same footing
with them; but the deep shadow I seek for my face
writhes like my body, endlessly shrinking,
though not from shame or revelation.
When the secret we sealed together is torn from its sheath,

oh, if only it were possible for them to see
my back drenched in sweat, the fearless chest
leaning over me, heart pumping like a bellows,
and in me that serpent shedding its skin,
oh, if only it would come from the earth
and take its fill of me.

XIII

Time will pass. And the times that pass
will crush to dust the blind stuff in us:
could my beauty, or his glory, stay?
My head leaning on my hand, my gaze lost
in the emptiness of this stone, are what will stay —
and this empty, worn-out tomb.
Royalty and beauty, nothing but dust!
Sightseers and bespectacled scholars
stroll around us in the museum all day.
Then darkness falls, the lights go out, extinguished
by the watchman: all night, each night, kept for us two.

XIV

I didn't believe that flame had died — you,
more godlike than all the gods, more manly than men:
the earth trembled at your touch
and toppled town and country,
my wells are far deeper now,
my deserts more scorching than your noonday sun;
if I have lived in blood on your loins
I await your return parched and sealed,
none dreams more fiercely of your sudden return,
the sudden spark you'll strike —
priceless the fire between us.

XV

You left, a single image in my mind.
Maybe you forgot which expedition or which land,
but you remembered the stranger in me:
astride your horse, was it my face you saw,
no, every syllable I spoke gave off heat from afar —
like the spark that flashed from your eye
at the touch of the wrong harp string:
in me you kept the king who wanted to escape himself
for an instant, stripped, headstrong, a distant

[92]

other, you stared at the horizon

and called from the room: come, saddle my horse, my queen.

XVI

A procession of women will circle the tomb

and none will know I was the last to come:

so weary, so eager to leave, for so long,

so long on fire with fear of being forgotten:

Look, there's life in my womb!

No sleep, no rest, the ritual underway

already in its black grief transforming us all to stone

forever untouchable in our solitude,

plucked from the tree and left to rot on a silver dish

the hand cannot reach — I'm young:

what will happen to the wild blood swirling in me?

XVII

You fell silent, the question coiled and writhed.

Was I a wife to you on moonless nights

or did we remain sister and brother,

as we were born? Now I alone know

our bodies didn't meet and the spirit

that flew far off to alight on a brittle branch.

I want it to live for ages, that curiosity, dark,

devouring, feeding on this deep doubt —

I who saw you, a sword at my side

half asleep, poised to unsheathe itself, and in me

a restless horde poised to drift your way.

XVIII

—translated in memory of Nazan Parer

A day to die will come, for me too,

and all those I have seen and heard

will go away: even if others live

this must be the last judgement on me:

my face in marble will wear away in weeping —

for I am all women and also none.

If I must stand drained of all line and color,

if I now stand mute and echoless,

know then the time will come

when none will see the last word on my face.

You look at me: gone is that instant, gone that breath.

SP-CE

SEYFÜLMÜLÜK
For a Portrait Study by FT

Let me spin a tale for you, Beloved,

let me recite you another, yet one more, story,

so that you may spend your thousand-and-one days,

                                   thousand-and-one nights

just so: as a sleepless, feverish, unmarred whole.

On the iridescent mother-of-pearl frame

stretch fine muslin gauze and embroider for me

in silk-wound gold wire and multicolored threads

a mansion, an exact likeness of the one

I drew by candlelight on the cave wall

of my deepest self, for you.

Keep my sorrow a secret, no one must hear,

no one must ever mock my love for a figure,

sketch out my face, in paint render my body

on fire in the blood that flows from me to you,

let me grasp you once more, stepping out of the picture:

may my hands burn as fiercely as my eye's pupil,

may my fountains rush and flow and the shadow of the chain

you strung around my neck rattle and groan,

for you, my beloved, let me become the male Sheherezade,

so that from new, entirely new, tales I may compose a unique parable,

may my inky letters flow into your figures,

if the tomorrow that awaits us is a winter as black as coal,

I am closer to your death even than you.

SP-MK

THE VERY WORDS OF FREEDMAN SİNAN

Night will end soon — my very last one,

morning will come soon — my very last one.

On this last morning the door of my cloudy story will shut,

floodwaters or air will erect an impregnable wall

against all that's happened.

My great sultan has issued his orders:

my architect who begrudged me my greatness,

he will be beaten to death,

his screams, rising from the Tower's depths,

will spread to every corner of my city,

the whole world will hear those terror-filled cries,

I who was never denied by wall or water,

let him come and stand upright before me,

let a thousand and one fists beat my Sinan mercilessly.

My God, what can this rage be — what fury

that boils over from the whirlpools in those dark eyes,

you might wonder if the Creator had willed

for my last night to be like coal, a pure blackness.

It's against You that my sultan takes his measure:

under Your look Byzantium's greatness melted,

how else could it be for a slave's slave?

Night will end soon and with it my life, my whole story:

a new one, blurred and gray, will stir from my ashes.

Blind stubbornness or blind faith or blind rebellion:
freeing the spirit held in my trust, yesterday
I surrendered this body, but freedom?
I had unbound myself long ago — what remains
is no less a ruin than the earth beneath me,
no less a void than the heavens above me.
Whoever strikes me, I won't utter a sound.
The instant they lop the hands from these wrists
I'm already dead.

SP-MK

WAKING INTERVAL

I woke up, Enis, and the moment I awoke
I saw that everything was a scene from a
dream: I was inside a book, a worm-eaten
volume: leather binding worn, spine faded,
a crack down the middle of a large expanse
turning from red to dark brown, a dank
musty smell rising from the paper. It hit me:
I wasn't the writer of the book, I *was* the book.
This is a case that staggers my imagination:
what used to happen only in my dreams
faces me now in my waking life. And hey,
since I'm letting you in on it, pretty soon
everyone's imagination is going to be
staggered: for those in the know will know that
my last breath expired fifteen years ago —
by then my book had long been finished.

Since that's how it is, dear Enis, my waking
likely came to pass in a dream of yours:
jog your mind, try to remember, please —
do we have a memory in common here,
or is it a trace that belongs to you alone?
Once you quoted Kant to me, as we sat
at some bar in broad daylight: *opus,*

non opera alterius, you said in passing —

how beautifully and justly you discoursed

on the subject of keeping hands off what

belongs to the poet. The other night I rose

from where I was lying and, once I cleared

the smoke of sleep away, found myself

in the book that was me. I wandered from line

to line at first, jumping quickly from one page

to the next, then slowed down and moved along

with less hurry — there must be something you'd

like to tell me, old friend: I'll wait here,

how can I go back to sleep?

Edip

CE-SSE

THE UNMADE BED

You wanted me to write you from every city
I visited, but I couldn't. Not because what
you wanted was silly or took much effort —
no, not at all: my aim was to get distance
on our life together. I'd spent my last ounce
of energy taking a leave from our relationship,
and what good would it have done to write you
from each city, besides adding one more knot
to the ties I wanted to loosen? I bought
this postcard at the museum as soon as I saw it
and carried it around with me in my purse.
It's only a handful of watercolors, Delacroix's
Unmade Bed, but it's genius on a tiny surface.
Of course I couldn't help recalling that
first night I came to Arnavutköy. You're
there now, I suppose, wrapping your arms
around your own rumpled self since I left:
likely all those lonely nights stacking up
down to this morning have made your bed
a long and endless tangle of restless sleep.

It was the Delacroix painting that made me
think of all these things. It would remind you
of other things, I'm sure — no doubt you'll see

the unmade bed as the mirror of our nights

together. I can't deny that my body's desires

were satisfied on it; but I'm a woman,

a being who, when her soul is starved,

slowly dries up, the empty half bit by bit

consuming the full half. Going from city

to city, hotel to hotel, I brooded on this:

you, deaf to my endless explaining, you, blind

to my restlessness, you, the impassive

audience of my sailing from the port —

I can't go back to that house, that bed —

if I'm to listen from now on to one person's

silence, I choose mine.

CE-SSE

ABDAL'S DREAM

That book of mine, he said, was set in a room where the walls, floor and ceiling were covered in mirrors. As it happened, no one saw that I wasn't there.

That was to be expected, though. Before it was written no one had felt the book's absence. Or, more precisely, no one had felt its lack — which may explain why, when and as the book was at last written, some could have sensed that it was just too much.

For some it falls short, he said; for others it's too much. It all starts when your wanting to secure a place so you can travel toward yourself takes on an imposing dimension.

And, behind that, beneath it, overshadowed, there lies the wish to seduce the place.

To sleep without a break, habitually, but to wake up one night in fits and starts, riddled with sleeplessness, to get up and place an irreplaceable object in an empty suitcase, as if, in the dark, you were letting a sentence drop on a blank sheet of paper, and then to go back to sleep.

In the morning, upon waking, to see that all the objects had vanished from the suitcase whose lid was left open, forgotten, the sentences on the paper piled up, the letters run together, the words knotted, illegible.

Remember your dreams, he said, keep a record of your nightmares, acquaint yourself with the weary, dead-winged angels who move with you through your sleep, get along with them.

Here you are, seduced by the place you thought you had seduced. Feel it: see if the place you secured hasn't secured a place inside you. If it has, a traveler will step into you, one whose eyes are gleaming ominously, one who intends to go far away.

Once I met such a runaway traveler. He'd been seen in Russia's deep valleys. He got off the train at a small mountain station in La Pampla, and for a long time he lived at the far end of the village in a house with a garden. Then he was seen on a train in Egypt, heading south.

He left traces on me. This habit of rolling tobacco dates from those years. And of pitching my tent on the shores of still lakes. Heart-searing silences accompany my *türkü* tunes. I turn my back to the sunset and watch the hills facing me.

The letters I sent him are all still in the bottom of his bag. General Delivery, Kentucky. c/o Yen-si, South China. The ones I received are in the drawer. I draw water from them sometimes. That takes the edge off my dryness. A traveler's flask engulfs all kinds of thirst.

In this cell, he said, I set the plot of his book: covering the walls are tallies of crime and injustice. Some people, after they wrote them, moved on; others faded out. All left behind a single, indivisible word. Just put your hand on the wall. It'll heave back its contents.

Winter has come, snow tumbles off the mountains, on its way down covering the trees and the rooftops, blocking the roads. When the white falls, our eyes turn to the horizon and we wait. We feel the warm breath of the wolves drawing close. The logs in the fire slowly empty themselves out. The moment the first speck appears in the distance, we're ready.

I've forgotten where my homeland is. Darkness has taken over the streets where I was born. The shutters of my home have long been closed. Birds no longer come to perch in my garden.

But it's been a long time since my memories called out to me, he said. As soon as I've found a horse, I'll return to my path. If it happens to be a mule, I'll mount the craggy heights, right to the top. It won't take me long to see all that I can.

A Time is born, an inking in of numerous other times. That dry leaf comes from the bank of a far-off stream, from a distant autumn. At the foot of a volcanic mountain I found this ash-colored stone. The strip of cloth is a keepsake from a woman who took me flying on her bosom.

No one can use the traces I've gathered. All I've lived through collects in my well alone. I lost my right eye at the scene of a hunt, crippled my hand in a cave, caught from the East the fever that enfolds my body each night. When I go out and walk among people, I can see that they understand nothing.

Another time, he said, we labored on a great construction, built walls and erected turrets on their four corners. At night, worn out, we lay down quietly on our mattresses and surveyed new lands in our sleep. Mornings, the sun invaded our eyes. We broke fast there, knocked open sharp onions to mix with our bread. When the building was almost finished we asked for leave and again set out.

Remember your dreams, you'd do well to forget what you've lived through, if Life goes on, if that has, or can have, any importance, good, get away from here. Wherever you arrive first, may the rain welcome you. Choose a different sleep for yourself then, find a dream for yourself that you've never had.

My path has dragged me off into different ages. I saw stones, came across ruins, temples, and cities, intact or razed. No one knew who had built a fortress wall. All had forgotten why a public square had been emptied out, abandoned. Coarse cloths were wrapped around chunks of wood, I remember, unengraved tombstones scattered across a plain. I saw horse bones, bronze masses, dry trees.

I have a *saz* with fourteen strings, a double neck and a deep womb, he said. When I camp for the night on the foot of a hill and build myself a fire, I pull the cover off my *saz*. I place my bag and gun at my feet. A tune that's been on my lips for many days descends into my fingertips, my calluses ache. Night creatures listen to me. My tunes scatter and drift far away. The unfathomable sadness inside me ebbs.

Soon, on the door of my cell a knock will be heard. I'll be offered hot soup by a familiar hand. I'll wait for my ink to dry, for sounds and images to shrink back into a corner, for a fine veil of steam to cover my reflection in the mirror. I've grown tired of chasing after myself, my blood has grown heavier, soon I'll be out on the streets of the city, atoms in a doomsday crowd, my soul.

SP-MK

FACE TO FACE CONVERSATION VIII

But I can also be seen as a stone, he said. Adamantine (hard to imagine otherwise), ice or burning coal, depending on the season (the outstretched hand will know), luminous (since it can both absorb and reflect), fearful: because it can break, does break, must once have been broken into pieces — once upon a time a whole contained all, solid, singular, thought to be indissoluble, what's left of it, me.

However, he said, smiling, I'm neither one, nor have I become the other, rather the midpoint between two states: the one I couldn't keep and the one I couldn't attain — left transitory, incomplete. Pay heed to the rain, try and read the stones wherever they appear to you: when two odd syllables connect a chance meaning may emerge.

SP-MK

FACE TO FACE CONVERSATION IX

I've always wanted to be one less than myself, he said: my fate decreed that I be one more. Didn't I pass this way before, didn't I leave a notch, now rubbed off, just here, on this big, white silent stone, on the top floor of that house I'd met a dark-skinned woman: aged, tired, complacent, she'd come from far away, settled in your midst, she called out to me one morning, using my full name even, knowing who I was, she declared to me with heartfelt sorrow that my day, my time, was up, I died, he said dryly, and after a few days turned to ashes, if I've suddenly come back it's because I forgot something: maybe a smell, a color, I don't remember so well now, maybe a word less or more.

SP-MK

from RESPONSE

I trailed after it with the endless refrain of a limping, broken tune inside me: as intricate meanings amassed in one tongue before me and in another behind, wingless, I soared between two hills, hesitant accents adorned my words, sounds hurled from afar, from strange lands, took cover in my voice, I saw rocks, clustered bits of wet, black stone, weeds too, spit from the sea, driven toward the shoreline between ebb and flow, I saw, all collected here to mete out the remains of a long silence: Time, wind, the quick decay of dead birds, motionless trees, a horde of dry cypress cones, and, far off, souls' Ocean.

SP-MK

DEAR BARTLEBY

You loved *Wakefield*, my young friend, and there's more
to it as well, if I'm not reading too much
into what you've written, you're overly affected
by my odd tale. "I was surprised,"
you're saying somewhere, but in truth it's you
who surprised me with your astonishing remark:
you plainly think I write what I live,
the lives woven into my books you see
as nectar gathered from my own days.
No! Don't be downhearted, the stale life you think
you lead is a hurricane next to the undeviating
flow of my hours. Friend, I never had a life.
And in view of the perfectly empty years
of the past, I never will: my body
is a boat adrift on a calm lake surrounded
by mountains: everything, yes everything,
begins and ends on the precarious stage
at the bottom of my mind. If I stopped
I'd go crazy, but I can't stop:
without letters tumbling down to my fingertips,
I'd have cracked up in nothing flat.

CE-SSE

NEGRESCO, 1915

Across the sea an irony made of stone:
it was built as a luxury hotel at the end
of the Peace. Now we're at the beginning
of the War: far off, the bullets are flying
like they mean to go on until there's just one
person left alive. I can't fall asleep at night.
In the candlelight I stare at my legs deserted
by their aching while I listen to the moans
filling up the rooms. The sea muttering
behind the shutters tells us this winter
will be harsher than ever. I know the sea
doesn't talk, at night it doesn't talk,
death has no words, Life alone can speak,
if it desires to speak: a few jolly tunes
shellshocked in the corners of the ballroom,
love whispers hiding breathlessly beneath my bed,
the floor attendant moving silently down
the corridor, now the nurse shushing me.

CE-SSE

THE ALGONQUIN

It's clear that he came here to live.
Before setting out, he found a sidewalk tour
of New York on the Internet and printed out
a selection from the dead season's programs:
Blue Note bar, De la Choncha Tobacco Shop,
concerts and exhibitions, priorities highlighted
with a green felt-tipped pen. And he came to write:
at the other end of the table, the stack of pages
torn from lined yellow notepads that he filled
one by one, the cramped letters in ink, precisely
aligned, some words, it appears, underlined
with a ruler: nothing there like deletions
to capture the eye, no sign of a pause in the flow
of writing. A few books in his mother tongue
that he'd brought with him, Frank O'Hara's
poems (purchased here, to judge from the notes
on the first few pages) and a biography of Capote —
these were lying beneath a city guide
and a folding map when we entered the room.

Any source you turned to for information
on our hotel would say the same things:
from the moment it opened in 1902
it's been a refuge for one-of-a-kind writers:

from Dorothy Parker to James Thurber, a row
of odd birds have made its rooms their nests.
When Faulkner heard he'd won the Nobel Prize,
he took Number 604 and wrote his Stockholm speech.
If you perused the register . . . festive dinners
in the Oak Room, mating cries from a forbidden fling
on the top floor, clink of glasses in the lobby,
a lone wolf with bloodshot eyes, who knows
why, stretched out between night and morning.
Our most distinguished regular, Mr. Simon,
still here after stepping off the ship
that pulled in nearly half a century ago, says
nothing like this ever happened here before,
the new waiter who went upstairs
for room service at midnight noticed it:
the newspaper he put in front of the door
each morning was still lying where he'd left it.

CE-SSE

FAR AWAY

This one's for you, a reconstituted version
of Ponte Vecchio. If I'm not mistaken,
in a past life you lived in one of those houses
hanging off the bridge. I took off my glasses,
brought the postcard to my nose, and examined
them one by one: if you ask me, the middle one
with three storeys and a red-brick facade
is the one most like you. Your kitchen
must have been in the foyer, the large-bottomed
woman should of course be named Beatrice:
a beauty who tired of giving birth to children
and looking after you — still, fervent moans
should be heard wafting from your bedroom
on the second floor. Your studio's on the roof,
it seems: your eyes mirror the dense water
of the Arno, you take in its thick melancholy
every day and think of me — far far away,
I'm in my own bedroom in my own house
on a gloomy street of Byzantium, my
husband pulled my nightgown up to my belly
and pushed in, still trying to chase you away —
but so many long years have gone by in between.

CE-SSE

[132]

GOING DOWN TO THE WATER

No, Vic, sweetheart, light of my life, even
for Kubilai Khan I couldn't get out of bed.
There's no sense of architecture left in me,
let alone a project. I'd sacrifice all my hair
to put two stones together. If I knew
of a single god who existed, I'd beg him
every day: please take away my sleep
so I can be rid of that nightmare
where I tear myself to pieces nonstop,
let me drift through my nights like a *djinn*,
I'm bone tired of that *ifrit* deep inside me.
Let my eyes be bowls of blood, my body melt
away, just save my soul from the claws of hell.
Write to me more often. Line some words up
on a pad in the morning and send them.
Give me the blood that I'll lose anyhow.
I'm alone by the water, the one voice I hear
the moment I awake is telling me,
"Fill your pockets with stones" —
I think I'm ready to let myself go.

                              Virgin

                                        CE-SSE

F MINOR — D-940

Of these two pianos one must surely be

the other's misgiving. Play it at night

before bed, it's blood, play it first thing in the morning,

one is the other's phantom. Naked, wet,

woman, how did it ever happen

that a man struck up these sounds:

of the two pianos, at least one feels broken.

SP-MK

D-810

In the all-night coffeehouse by the seashore
the young girl sits listening to "Death and the Maiden"
through her headset. The searing notes Schubert strung together
spread out through her frail, slender body.
Sitting at a table in the other corner, Death:
so quiet there's nothing to see but its silence.

SP-MK

PURE CONVERSATIONS I

Freezing in mid-step, he says, it's as if I'd banned
the joy of life from my presence. We're at neither
a light nor a crossing, we're standing still
in the middle of the sidewalk. If we had a destination
I'd think we were halfway there, but we don't:
we're in a scene frozen in time. I'm almost ashamed,
he proceeds, even of the little everyday pleasures.
If my eye lights on the small women I like
and my skin comes alive with goosebumps,
I fall suddenly into old sorrows that steal
out from unfamiliar places and fill me up,
if I listen to a lively Boccherini quintet
I find in my memory a gull swooping
away by night on rustling wings, a
tightly knotted yarn of agony left behind —
one of every two steps I take is shackled.

CE-SSE

PURE CONVERSATIONS II

Poppies, for instance, have no reason to be.
It was the beginning of summer, the middle
of a wide valley, the train flowing through fields
peeling away from the tracks: I saw them
and knew, suddenly, they're the reason I am,
they're the reason I was there.

CE-SSE

PURE CONVERSATIONS III

It was night, we stayed a long time out
on the balcony that overhung emptiness
like a precarious crag, then, face turned
toward the expanse of water, he said,
"Do you know what 'water of life' means?"
Partly it was the distraction and partly
the challenge of a question that didn't give
itself away that pulled me in. I turned and
looked at him almost in awe. He'd got me.
He smiled. "I heard it from a gardener friend
who once brought me a passion flower.
He shaped the soil in the pot with his hands,
then put in the plant. He felt called on
to explain, as he poured in lots of water:
'The water of life is for things uprooted.'"

CE-SSE

PURE CONVERSATIONS IV

When summer came that year I headed north,
along the coast where sharp rocks with black faces
thrust into the open sea half aimlessly
I wandered. Do you know what it means
to hit the road half aimlessly? — it means
the other half is still more aimless. Once
when I passed through the dim silent streets
of a town I'd stopped at and reached
the main square, thick clouds filled the sky
and I took shelter under an awning,
in my headphones Carissimi's *Jonas* oratorio.
A few glasses of rum came and went at my table.
Why from the first day that weird prophet's
been fidgeting in me who knows, just when
I want to get away from myself a big fish
swallows my body, rushes back to the shore
I broke away from, and vomits.

If I can never erase that day from my mind,
it's not because of the sudden cloudburst that
fell on the multitudes jammed into the square
and sent them running like it was doomsday.
Summer rains rain everywhere alike, the huge
drops wink in and out of the sun chasing them,

everybody races to the eaves, first comes

the fresh air on your face, then the deep smell

unites with it. That day too the rain came and went.

I took off my headphones and looked around

half aimlessly. To this day I haven't forgotten:

the invisible army of sparrows that filled to bursting

the huge and leafy linden tree in the middle

of the square had struck up, after the rain,

a rain chorus: birds want to be rain, they do.

CE-SSE

NOTES TO SELECTED POEMS

"Modern Times": *abdal* has complex connotations in Turkish folk culture and poetic tradition. Broadly it may be described as a wandering poet-mystic who has renounced wordly affairs. Historically, it is an epithet adopted by folk poets of Alevî or Bektaşî affiliation, such as Pîr Sultan Abdal.

"The High Pastures": "Yassıada" is the island off Istanbul where several high government officials, including the prime minister, were imprisoned, tried, and hanged after a military coup in 1960.

"Passport": Enis Batur explains the background to the poem in an essay by the same title in his *Seyrüsefer Defteri*, İstanbul, Yapı Kredi Yayınları, 1997, pp.86-98.

"Migratory Bird": the poem refers to Ahmet Hamdi Tanpınar (1901-1962) poet, novelist, literary historian; and his mentor, fellow poet Yahya Kemal Beyatlı (1884-1958

"Fugue XVII": *dîvan* is the name given to a collection of poetry in traditional Ottoman literature. The term also appears in "Conversing with Attar" (see below).

"At Sâdî's Graveside": Sâdî of Shiraz (1184-1291), Persian poet, wrote *Gülistan* (The Rose Garden) and *Bustan* (The Fruit Garden).

"Conversing with Attar": Fariduddin-i Attar (d.ca.1230), Persian poet. The numbers "740-746; 4869-4901" following the title of the poem indicate lines in *The Conference of the Birds*, Attar's mystical masterpiece.

"Digenis": Thomas Whittemore (1871-1950), founder of the Byzantine Institute of America in 1930, who initiated and led the restoration of the mosaics in the Hagia Sophia and the Chora. Enis Batur's essay (in *Seyrüsefer Defteri*, İstanbul, Yapı Kredi Yayınları, 1997, pp. 70-85) revealed in print for the first time Whittemore's correspondence with Henri Matisse, whose two charcoal portraits are included among the documents traced by Batur. In the poem, the reader will also find references to brother-artists Abidin and Arif Dino, to Abidin's wife Güzin, literary critic and translator, and to Samih Rifat, architect and photographer with whom Enis Batur shot a documentary in Paris.

"Doomsday Verse": "X, 8-9" refers to the relevant chapter and verse in the *Kur'an*.

"Elegies: The Sarcophagus of Mourning Women": "the Sarcophagus of Mourning Women stands in the Hall of Sidonian Sarcophagi in the İstanbul Museum of Archaeology. According to the Mendel Catalogue, it is Ionian in style, sculpted ca. 350 BC by a Sidonian who was influenced by Attic art. The artist, once thought to be of Lycian origin, was probably from an Aegean island or coastal town, as the sarcophagus is different from Lycian works in composition and spirit.

The poem was sparked by Samih Rifat's illustrated article on the sarcophagus; his article was inspired by Onat Kutlar's essay, 'Epitaph for an Eastern King.' The poem has no organic links, however, with either of these pieces or with the authoritative description in the Mendel

Catalogue. I looked at the sculptures and composed. Is it necessary to see, to have seen, the Sarcophagus of Mourning Women? I don't think so: the poem depends no more on the sarcophagus in the museum than on any other sarcophagus still buried, perhaps never to be found." (Enis Batur, endnote to the first publication of the original in 1993.)

"Seyfülmülük": the title refers to the first story in *The Thousand and One Nights* with Seyfülmülük as the hero.

"The Very Words of Freedman Sinan": Freedman Sinan was an architect who served Mehmed the Conqueror (1430-1481).

"Waking Interval": "Edip" refers to Edip Cansever (1928-1985), one of the leading poets of the Second New movement.

"Abdal's Dream": see note on "Modern Times."

EDITOR'S NOTE

This translation project was begun by Saliha Paker and Clifford Endres in 1994, continued by Endres and Selhan Savcıgil-Endres over the next decade, and completed with the collaboration of Mel Kenne.

The present selection follows a more or less chronological order and is drawn mainly from two major volumes of poetry by Enis Batur: *The East-West Dîvan* (1997), a collection of dramatic poems written between 1988 and 1996, and *Papyrus, Ink, Quill* (2002), a personal selection of lyric, dramatic, and short epic poems that span thirty years: 1972-2002.

The earliest poems here are "Modern Times" (1982) and "A Talisman and Tragedy" (1984). These are followed by poems from *The Gray Dîvan*, represented here in translations by Endres and Savcıgil-Endres. *The Gray Dîvan* was initially published in book form in 1990 and incorporated later into *The East-West Dıvan*. Similarly, "Elegies: The Sarcophagus of Mourning Women" came out in Turkish in 1993 and was subsequently included in *Papyrus, Ink, Quill*; these poems were the first of this selection to be translated.

The current volume also covers some of Enis Batur's work published after 2002: "Abdal's Dream," an important sequence of prose poems is presented here in its entirety, together with three other poems from the eponymously titled collection (2003). These are followed by a representative selection from the Turkish of *The Divan of Aggravating Circumstances* (2003) and a few uncollected poems.

I owe special thanks to Enis Batur for years of challenge, encouragement, and appreciation.

[144]

I would also like to thank Coşkun Yerli and Ronald Tamplin for permission to include their fine translation of "Digenis," Barbaros Altuğ for opening the way for publication, and the Turkish Ministry of Culture for its generous financial support of poetry in translation.

TURKISH SOURCES

Enis Batur, *Doğu-Batı Dîvanı*. İstanbul, Yapı Kredi Yayınları, 1997.

----------, *Papirüs, Mürekkep, Tüy. Seçme Şiirler 1973-2002*. İstanbul, Yapı

Kredi Yayınları, 2002.

----------, *Abdal Düşü. Düzyazı Şiirler 1998-2002*. İstanbul, Altıkırkbeş

Yayın, 2003.

----------, *Ağırlaştırıcı Sebepler Dîvanı*. İstanbul, Altıkırkbeş Yayın, 2003.

Kitap-lık, March 2003. No. 59. İstanbul, Yapı Kredi Yayınları, 2003.

Gece Yazısı, October 2003, No. 3. İstanbul, Sel Yayıncılık.

BIOGRAPHICAL NOTES

Enis Batur (b. 1952), one of the most prolific of contemporary Turkish poets, was educated at the Lycée St. Joseph in Istanbul, attended Middle East Technical University in Ankara, and completed his studies in Paris. Between 1973, when his first collection of poems came out, and 2006, he published twenty-four books of poetry, twenty-seven volumes of essays, three novels, five travelogues, and an autobiography. Translations of Batur's poetry have been published in Italian, Persian, French, Flemish, and Corsican; two of his novels have also appeared in French translation – *L'amer savoir* (2002) and *La pomme* (2005). Poetry and essays have won Batur several prizes in Turkey, and *Imago Mundi* (1999), his second book of poems in Italian translation, was awarded the Sibilla Aleramo Prize for Poetry.

Since his return to Turkey in the late 1970s, Batur has been founding editor and editor-in-chief of a number of influential literary magazines and journals. He has contributed to publications too numerous to cite, produced radio and television programs, curated exhibitions of modern French and Spanish painting, and from 1988 to 2005, served as executive board member of Yapı Kredi Culture, Arts and Publishing House. Here, he was responsible for the publication of the masters of Turkish literature and of world classics in translation, bringing about an unprecedented literary and cultural renaissance in Turkish private publishing.

Enis Batur lives in Istanbul with his wife, the painter Fatma Tülin, and teaches at Galatasaray University. He has a son by his first marriage.

Clifford Endres and Selhan Savcıgil-Endres live in Istanbul, where they established the Department of American Culture and Literature at Kadir Has University in 2000. Clifford Endres first came to Turkey as a Fulbright lecturer in 1985, and has taught at Boğaziçi, Ege, and Başkent universities. He is the author of *Joannes Secundus: The Latin Love Elegy in the Renaissance* (1982), *Austin City Limits* (1987), and articles in such periodicals as *Renaissance Quarterly*, *Southwest Review*, *Chicago Review*, and *Texas Monthly*. Selhan Savcıgil-Endres has taught at Hacettepe and Başkent universities and has written on various Turkish and American authors, including Orhan Pamuk and Paul Auster. Their translations have appeared in a variety of journals and anthologies, many of which are listed in the Acknowledgements of the present volume.

Mel Kenne is a poet who teaches in the American Culture and Literature department at Kadir Has University in Istanbul. He has many publications to his credit, including three books of poetry and a compact disk he produced with composer Patrick Boland, entitled *The Book of Ed*. As a translator, he has rendered into English the work of a number of Latin American, Spanish and Turkish poets. He and Saliha Paker translated Latife Tekin's novel *Dear Shameless Death* (2001).

Saliha Paker is Professor of Translation Studies in the Department of Translation and Interpreting Studies at Boğaziçi University, Istanbul, and an Honorary Research Fellow of the Centre for Byzantine, Ottoman and

Modern Greek Studies, University of Birmingham. Her research has been focused on Ottoman and modern Turkish translation history and on translated Turkish literature. Her work in English includes an edited volume, *translations: (re)shaping of literature and culture* (Boğaziçi University Press, 2002), various essays in international publications, *Nar '96*, a bilingual edition of contemporary Turkish writing (with Senay Haznedaroğlu, Oğlak Yayınları, 1996), and joint translations of modern Turkish poetry as well as fiction by Latife Tekin: *Berji Kristin Tales from the Garbage Hills* (with Ruth Christie) and *Dear Shameless Death* (with Mel Kenne), both published by Marion Boyars.

Ronald Tamplin taught for many years at universities in New Zealand, France, Turkey but most of his time at Exeter University in England, where he is now Honorary University Fellow. His books include studies of T.S. Eliot, Seamus Heaney, and poetic rhythm. He also writes on painting. As a poet he is widely published, has two collections and won a number of prizes. He has collaborated in translating from Hungarian and Georgian, but especially from Turkish, working with Coşkun Yerli.

Coşkun Yerli is a poet and translator of poetry by Eavan Boland, Roger McGough, Henry Read, Matsuo Bashō and Kobayashi Issa. He has also translated much of J.D. Salinger's fiction into Turkish, and Turkish poetry into English, including his own, with Ronald Tamplin.

Designed by
Samuel Retsov

■

Text and titles: Centaur

■

acid-free paper

■

Printed by
The Country Press